CODEP

CODEPENDENCY

HOW TO
BREAK FREE AND LIVE
YOUR OWN LIFE

DAVID STAFFORD
AND
LIZ HODGKINSON

PIATKUS

© 1991 David Stafford and Liz Hodgkinson

First published in 1991 by
Judy Piatkus (Publishers) Ltd,
5 Windmill Street, London W1P 1HF

This edition published in 1998

A catalogue record for this book is
available from the British Library

ISBN 0–7499–1834–9

Set in Linotron Ehrhardt by
Wyvern Typesetting Ltd, Bristol
Printed and bound in Great Britain by
Biddles Ltd, Guildford and King's Lynn

About the Authors

Sadly **David Stafford** died in October 1997 of a heart attack. A psychoanalytic psychotherapist in private practice, he was for several years Director of the St Joseph's Centre in Haslemere, Surrey. He also supervised the work of the Drug and Alcohol Rehabilitation Clinic, Guildford, an NHS facility, for South West Surrey Health Authority. He was a psychology graduate of Brunel University and his background included voluntary work with down and outs with the Simon Community, intensive crisis intervention work with the Arbours Association in North London and residential social work in several therapeutic communities for the Richmond Fellowship including their specialist drug unit. David carried out research in Social Services and Education and his previous publication as a joint author was *An Agreed Understanding*, NFER Nelson, 1987. It looks at parent-professional communication in relation to children with special educational needs. In 1992 he wrote *Children of Alcoholics*, published by Piatkus.

David was born in Dublin, where he spent his formative years. He was married with three children. Besides his family and his work, David's principal preoccupation was with the fortunes of Queens Park Rangers Football Club. He was a keen football fan.

David entered a helping profession only after overcoming considerable personal problems. He reached his own personal 'rock bottom' at 19 years of age. It took six years and a considerable amount of professional and other help for him to build proper bridges back to normal living. David drew on his own personal experiences and how he grew from them to inform his professional practice. He believed that it is only by the grace of God, and the love and care of ordinary loving relationships that true healing can take place. He was always grateful for the love and companionship of his wife Sue, for the tremendous example of faith in adversity demonstrated by his mother, and the memory of the love of his father who died far too early to be truly known, and before he could be healed.

David was a founding member of the National Association for Children of Alcoholics.

Liz Hodgkinson is a medical writer and regular contributor to national newspapers and magazines. She is the author of thirty-five books on medical and social issues, including *Sex is Not Compulsory*, *The Alexander Technique*, *Unholy Matrimony*, *Reincarnation — The Evidence*, and *Spiritual Healing*.

St Joseph's Centre for Addiction
Holy Cross Hospital

St Joseph's Centre, Holy Cross Hospital, Haslemere, is run by the Congregation of the Daughters of the Cross, a Roman Catholic Order dedicated to the provision of health and educational services. St Joseph's Centre is a registered charity, and offers services to appropriate people irrespective of race, religion or creed. As it is a non-profit making organisation, donations to further this work are welcomed.

Since this book was originally published in 1991, the St Joseph's Centre has expanded considerably to include a counselling clinic and a post-traumatic stress disorder programme.

The views on spirituality expressed in this book are not those of the Congregation of the Daughters of the Cross.

Contents

Acknowledgements

For expert help and information, Liz Hodgkinson would like to
thank Dr Michael Gormley, Dr Sandra Buchanan, Dr Diana Samways,
Hilary Henriques and Maya Parker.

David Stafford is enormously grateful to the Congregation of the
Daughters of the Cross for their patience, forbearance, and financial
support, which has made the St Joseph's project possible; Dr Tony Baker
who has inspired and challenged us; Richard Gill, Lindi Kornblum, Pat
Hack, Joan Thompson, Mavis Toyne, Lyn Walker, Mags Lewis, Sister
Nuala Kilmartin, Debbie Goddard, Carole Woodington, Sister Mary
Edmund, Kate and Hilary Henriques, Theresa Jordon, Barbara Mizzen,
Robert and Eva Gottesman, Penny Jeffcote, Belinda Bray, Ann Whatley,
Kay Clement, Gillian Moore, Kity Rohrbach, James Butler, Anthony John-
son, Lorraine Delvard, Tricia Payne, Ann Brackley, Ivy Blackman and
Ursula Harris, who have all made significant contributions to the work of
St Joseph's.
    Special thanks are due to Dr Bruce Lloyd and Bobby Lloyd, John Dane,
Maya Parker, Nicholas Lewis, Dr Sandra Buchanan, Myrna Gower, John
Southgate, Kate White, Peter Pugh, Lyn Buess, Annie McCaffrey, Chloe
Frankl, Andy Scott, Tony Reilly, Dr Diana Samways and many other
professionals who came to St Joseph's to share their ideas and their work in
1990.
    This book will have failed miserably if you leave it just with the memory
of the painful things expressed in it. Addicts, alcoholics and other
codependents give a wonderous testimony to the indomitability of the
human spirit, and the courage which it is possible to find in the face of
overwhelming odds. The biggest acknowledgement of all is due to the

xii

many alcoholics, addicts and other codependents who in treatment shed their roles and their masks to embrace the pain and the shame they had so dedicated their lives to hiding from themselves and others. To their surprise they discovered that they were not alone and could come to value and cherish the person they are, faults and all. Having discovered their strength, hope and honesty they began to make choices beyond that of mere survival. It has been a privilege for me to have stayed with people whilst they gave up in despair and reached their 'rock bottom', and then were paradoxically set free through surrendering to their illness. It has been a privilege to have been the first to get to know many a frightened and mistrustful child-within-the-adult, and to have helped to facilitate their integration into the whole person.

Finally, Liz and I are both grateful to Gill Cormode of Piatkus Books for her helpful comments and support.

Identities within the case histories have been changed to preserve confidentiality.

What is codependency?

If you have not come across the word before, *codependency* perhaps conjures up a cosy, healthy picture of togetherness, of *inter*dependence. But actually, the term denotes the opposite – unhealthy, unproductive and even self-destructive ways of relating to other people. It first came into being in America, about 10 years ago, to describe the behaviour of spouses or partners of alcoholics and other addicts.

Through intensive work with chemically dependent people and their families, doctors and therapists realised that people who partnered or sought out addicts very often did so because of severe and addictive-like problems of their own. It was noticed that, although partners and relatives often appeared extremely caring and supportive, the alcoholic, gambler, drugs or food abuser got no better for their devoted care. In fact, they usually became progressively worse.

One reason for this was (and is) that, instead of helping the addict to give up the substance, those around them unwittingly did everything possible to enable them to continue with their self-damaging behaviour.

At first, these well meaning people, now known as 'codependents', were called 'enablers'. They would always welcome back an alcoholic from a drunken bout, feed and clothe a heroin addict, make sure a gambler had a hot meal, a home and money. 'Enabling' battered wives would frequently

1

allow a husband addicted to violence back into the home, believing – or at least wanting to believe – his promises that abuse would never be inflicted upon them again.

WIDESPREAD PHENOMENON

After studying the phenomenon in addiction and detoxification centres, mainly in America, doctors realised that codependent behaviour had far wider implications than was first thought. Although it often manifested itself around some form of chemical dependency, codependency could also surface when there was no substance abuse of any kind. Furthermore, this type of relationship behaviour was extremely widespread in society. In fact, it was being claimed that it was epidemic the world over – and getting worse.

Codependents are how we describe those people who depend on others for their own sense of self-esteem. They are the over-supportive wives and loyal secretaries. They are – or can be – dedicated doctors and tireless social workers. Not that there is anything wrong with being supportive or loyal, but such behaviour becomes codependent when it is misplaced, when balanced judgment is lost, and the support or loyalty continues when it is not deserved, or appropriate. For example, a codependent secretary will always be willing to work overtime without pay, undertake extra duties – and put her own life in abeyance while serving her boss, who may take all the credit for her hard work, perhaps without even a 'thank you'.

Codependents, essentially, are people who cannot live their own lives. They live vicariously, have no real sense of their own identity and don't really know who they are.

They are like chameleons, taking their colours from their surroundings. Above all, they desperately want to be loved, needed and highly regarded.

A codependent could be you, your mother, your father, teacher or doctor. In fact, we probably all have at least a touch of codependency in us; we have all wanted to be needed at times, just as most of us have occasionally experienced feelings of anger, lust, greed, jealousy.

Codependency is never a positive characteristic and hurts

all it touches; many millions of people let codependency rule their lives. They attempt to control and manipulate others, by whatever means they can. They can't say no, and they let others walk all over them. They are the parents who won't let their children grow up, the wife who won't let her husband out of her sight in case he has an affair, the loyal worker who allows herself or himself to be exploited.

Codependents are people-pleasers, always putting others first at the expense of themselves. Initially, they may seem extremely caring, loving and self-sacrificing. But always, beneath the apparent saintliness, they seek to control others.

Codependents are the world's supreme looker-afterers, the copers, the eternal optimists who always know that better days are just ahead. They will tell you that things 'are not so bad', that 'it's getting better' – even when it is patently obvious that their world is crashing about their ears.

Some codependents are extremely nice people. Others can be absolutely horrible. They can keep you waiting for ages, be completely unreliable, make promises they never fulfil, be bullies, sadists or sexaholics. Also every abuser of alcohol, food or illicit drugs is a codependent.

RELATIONSHIP ADDICTS

Codependents are relationship addicts, and they can come from all classes of society. The condition flourishes equally in a council flat or a stately home. It affects both sexes, and has nothing to do with standards of education, intelligence or social background.

Because codependents do not have a strong personal sense of identity, and possess little sense of self-worth, they over-identify with their roles and relationships. Instead of being a woman who also happens to be a mother, a codependent with children will see herself first and foremost as a 'mother', not realising that this is only a role she assumes, albeit an important one. Another codependent may see himself as a politician first, and a human being second.

Compulsive in everything they do, they rush headlong into relationships which, inevitably, go wrong. They may be compulsive workaholics or drinkers, hobbyists, over-achievers.

Some never really fit in anywhere. They feel so empty inside that they constantly have to 'fill' themselves up with a ceaseless round of activity.

If you are severely codependent, it will eventually lead to illness, and continuous, unlifting depression is often an outward sign of the condition. These people become ill because, however hard they try, however self-sacrificing, high-achieving or workaholic they may be, they never gain any sense of satisfaction, never know when to stop. It seems as if the harder they try to 'fill' the yawning gap inside, the bigger it grows. Also, inwardly, codependents are full of rage, anger, hostility and resentment towards people who don't appreciate them enough; they feel exploited. They suffer great stress – and we all know that stress is responsible for many physical, mental and emotional illnesses.

Codependents don't like themselves very much – and they have no idea how to start loving their essential selves, or how to achieve a better sense of self-esteem.

Like all compulsions, codependency is a progressive condition – it will get steadily worse unless it is addressed. It won't clear up of its own accord. And because it is so debilitating, with so many negative reverberations, it needs to be replaced with healthy ways of relating. Otherwise, it is passed on from generation to generation.

Although the word used to describe it is relatively new, the condition has been known for centuries. Many of our greatest authors intimately understood the dangers of codependency, and wrote about it with feeling and sympathy. Writers as different as Shakespeare, Dickens, Thomas Hardy, D. H. Lawrence and George Eliot all wrote about destructive, codependent relationships. King Lear is a codependent, so is Lady Macbeth.

LEARNED BEHAVIOUR

So how does codependency start? Well, we still do not know all the answers, but we have learned enough about the dynamics of the phenomenon to be reasonably certain of its origins and ramifications.

Although there may be hereditary factors, social factors

mean that it is passed down from parents to their children in everyday interaction. Nobody is actually born codependent. Codependency is learned behaviour which has its origin in destructive and dysfunctional family relationships. These are the families where there is a lot of covering up and pretence, where nothing is what it seems. Many such families harbour what they regard as a shameful secret – perhaps Dad drinks a lot or gambles, or Mum is on tranquillisers. There may be rows, escalating into violence. Perhaps, more devastatingly, there is sexual abuse. Maybe there is a drug addict in the family.

Most families have skeletons in the cupboard, but in homes which breed codependency the skeletons are not allowed to come out; help is not sought. Because children from such a background feel they have to pretend that everything is all right, they are always on their guard, and never learn to relax and be themselves. So, they grow up never having learned how to be themselves, or even what their true identity is.

This is why, in adulthood, there is over-identification with other people, or with particular roles, jobs or professions – those which enable people to 'lose' themselves, to submerge themselves, especially attract codependents. Acting – hiding behind other people's lines, assuming – is an extremely codependent profession. So are the caring professions: medicine, social work, the Church. Codependents basically focus on other people's problems to avoid having to look at their own. They try to change others but never attempt to change themselves. Codependents are people who say, or at least think: I'd be all right if only everybody else changed.

This is not to say that all actors and actresses, all members of the caring professions are codependent – but such jobs do tend to attract people already possessing these tendencies. Above all, codependents need somebody or something to focus upon and hide behind. They are terrified otherwise that the real them might be revealed – and they are desperately ashamed of their real persona.

As you may have gathered, codependency is an extremely complicated condition. The purpose of this book is to explain it as clearly as possible in all its guises – and to suggest strategies for replacing it with a healthier way of relating to the world.

As the roots of codependency go very deep, it is not always easy to extricate yourself. People who come from severely dysfunctional backgrounds may start blaming their parents – but this does no good. After you've apportioned blame, everything remains exactly the same. And if your parents were themselves codependent or dysfunctional, the chances are that they were brought up in such a home. Like you therefore, they simply learned no other way of living. They thought that they were doing their best and that everybody in the family was 'coping' with the situation.

But as the condition is so easily passed down through the generations, possibly worsening, it is important that it is stopped somewhere. Until very recently, codependency was extremely difficult to treat as few professional therapists had received relevant training, and there were no treatment centres or self-help groups. Now, all this is changing; codependency is increasingly being recognised as a progressive illness, intimately related to addictions of all kinds. For this reason, much of the self-help and professional help available has developed out of addictive studies.

ST JOSEPH'S CENTRE FOR ADDICTION

St Joseph's Centre for Addiction in Haslemere, Surrey, where David Stafford is Director, has been in the forefront of research and service development in the field of codependency in the UK. The Centre was established in 1986 by the Congregation of the Daughters of the Cross, a Catholic order of nuns who have been running a hospital in Haslemere since 1917. Until 1986, the Sisters had a small ward set aside in the hospital for alcohol detoxification, but it became apparent that detoxification alone only briefly interrupted the illness of alcoholism. Left untreated, the alcoholic eventually resumed a destructive drinking pattern.

The establishment of the St Joseph's unit signalled a more intensive and determined effort to break the endless drink-detox-drink-detox cycle. Since its inception in 1986, the Centre has taken the view that the alcoholic or chemically dependent person cannot be treated in isolation. It is vital to understand where the drinking, or drug using, fits into the addict's overall personality, and, moreover, where the alcoholic or chemically dependent person fits into the family system and social network.

It is because of this concern for the person in the context of his or her whole life that St Joseph's quickly came to understand the phenomenon of codependency. The Centre employs a variety of methods, applied by a multidisciplinary team, to help the drug and alcohol dependent person *and their family* into recovery. Above and beyond any individual method, the Centre is committed to applying the 12 steps of Alcoholics Anonymous and other related 12-step programmes.

TWELVE STEPS TO SELF-HELP

The basis of many self-help groups is the 12-step programme first developed by Alcoholics Anonymous nearly 50 years ago. These steps have stood the test of time, and have shown themselves to be more successful for recovery than any other method.

Many people who recognise themselves as codependent will gain all the help and support they need from self-help groups. Others will need skilled professional help.

For most people, recognising codependency is acutely painful, because the condition flourishes on denial, as do all addictions. We all know the alcoholic's definition of an alcoholic – somebody who drinks more than he or she does. Codependents find it quite easy to recognise the condition in others, but less easy to spot in themselves.

Unravelling the complex relationships that codependency has made can be quite difficult. But it is always worth putting oneself through the process of recovering. In codependency, one is caught in a vortex of inappropriate behaviour which can get out of control, and which stops life from being in any way enjoyable. In this book we show you how to recognise even slight traces of codependency – and how to address them before they can build up. Those people who have small traces of codependency can probably recover just by understanding the problem, and we give some special advice in Chapter 4. But more severe cases will need structured help, whether self-help or from a professional therapist.

All the things worth having in life – happiness, self-esteem, a high sense of self-worth – are impossible while codependent attitudes remain. Even a modicum of codependency can sabotage success and achievement of maximum potential. So this book is for:

- Anybody who has ever allowed somebody else's behaviour to control them or affect them adversely.
- Anybody who is married to an addict, or has an addict child.
- Anybody who feels compelled to work and work and work.
- All those people who find it difficult to say no.
- Those who tend to think that others are more important than they are.
- Anybody who, personally, has been caught in the grip of an addiction.

It is also for anyone curious to know exactly what codependency is – because to know about the condition makes clear many things about people which previously may have seemed mysterious or inexplicable. Why, for instance, do some people complain about having to look after an elderly relative – and then when the relative dies, immediately find themselves somebody else old and infirm to care for? The answer is, because they're codependent!

Part One

UNDERSTANDING THE PROBLEM

1 | Five stories of everyday folk

Codependency has been described as 'a way of getting your needs met that doesn't get your needs met.' Does this sound like a contradiction in terms?

Take a look at these five stories about everyday codependent folk – and see if you can spot the pattern that is making life difficult, even unliveable in some cases, for each of them. Ask yourself, too, whether it strikes any chords in you.

SUSAN – THE SUPPORTIVE WIFE

Susan, 58, had been married for 32 years to Richard, an international engineer, and they had three grown-up children who had all left home. Susan was devastated when Richard told her that he had fallen in love with a much younger woman, his secretary, and wanted a divorce so he could marry the girl.

'How could he do this to me?' Susan asked herself as she cried herself to sleep. She had always been a supportive wife. She had dedicated her life to Richard, helping him in his career, being loyal and loving.

Richard's work had taken him all over the world and Susan always went with him, entertaining his business contacts, being the ever-smiling, perfect hostess at dinner parties and receptions. She thought they had a happy marriage, and her

11

her friends thought so, too. Richard was certainly the envy of many of his colleagues. Susan's world fell apart when Richard told her he had never really loved her and that, instead of being a proper human being, she was a 'cardboard cut-out'.

Her three children were very upset at their father's cruel remarks, and told him so. They also told him that he had no right to speak to their mother in such a way, and that, if anything, it was he who was the cardboard cut-out. They reminded Richard that their mother had given up everything, including the possibility of a career as a pianist, to look after him and go with him all over the world. Would he have been so successful, they asked, if she hadn't looked after him so well? Their words fell on indifferent ears.

Susan wanted to go to marriage guidance, but Richard refused to accompany her. As far as he was concerned, he said, the marriage was over – and he was more than pleased. She became extremely depressed and was eventually referred for psychotherapy.

PENNY – MOTHER'S LITTLE HELPER

Penny's mother had always been extremely difficult. She developed a drinking problem when her husband left her for a younger woman. Penny and her sister Anthea were young teenagers at the time. Nobody ever talked about Mother's drinking, and the two girls tried to pretend that it didn't happen. As the problem worsened, they stopped asking friends round to the house, in case they found Mother drunk and incapable.

Anthea left home at the earliest possible opportunity to go to University, and then married, moving away to another part of the country. She hardly ever visited her mother and rarely kept in touch.

Penny was different. Less academic than Anthea, she had always felt it was her responsibility to look after Mother and to protect her. After leaving school at 16 with a few O levels, Penny took a secretarial course and got a job in a solicitor's office in her home town, so that she could stay and look after Mother – somebody had to. As the years went by, Mother became ever more demanding, querulous, obstinate, jealous and possessive. She hated Penny to go anywhere, especially in the evenings after work. Eventually, Penny felt she had no choice but to give up her job to look after Mother. Her only remaining outlet was going to church.

After 10 years of this self-imposed restriction, Mother died, and everybody thought that Penny would at last have some life of her own. But no – six months later she married a man with multiple sclerosis who was confined to a wheel-chair. Bill needed almost constant round-the-clock care, and so Penny still could not go back to work. Anthea told her sister in no uncertain terms that she was daft, but Penny said: 'Bill needs me.'

The effort of looking after Bill on her own made Penny ill. She suffered several bouts of severe depression, and was prescribed tranquillisers. Now, at the age of 50, she is dependent upon tranquillisers, and although she wants to come off them, she blesses them for making her life tolerable. Bill is at least as difficult as Mother was, demanding, self-centred, possessive. He hates Penny to go anywhere, and friends feel she is completely under his thumb, even though he is physically so incapable.

CAROLINE – THE WRONGED WIFE

Caroline knew when she married Tim that he was a bit of a womaniser. He was a very attractive man, a high-earning stockbroker, tall, dark and handsome. No wonder she fell for him. She was very surprised when he seemed to be equally attracted to her, and took it as a sign that he would reform. All he needs is the love of a good woman, she told herself.

Caroline had some grounds for optimism: she had done well at school, and qualified as a solicitor. When she and Tim met, she was earning a good salary and looked like a real high flier. However, it wasn't long after they got married that Tim started having affairs. When Caroline found out, he assured her that they meant nothing, that he couldn't help it if he was highly sexed. He hinted that no one woman could satisfy him. Caroline began to wonder whether she might be undersexed, and whether this was why Tim could not seem to stop being unfaithful. He was right when he said the affairs meant nothing – they were mainly one-night stands.

After one blistering row, when Caroline found lipstick stains on his collar and a hotel bill for two in his pocket, Tim broke down and assured her that he would change, that this had been a lesson to him (Caroline had threatened to leave him). But she could not feel confident, although for a long time there was no further evidence.

As they grew more prosperous, they decided to sell their London flat and move to a house in the country. They would both commute to work. But Caroline suspected that Tim was having affairs again, and felt the only way of saving their marriage was to give up her job to become a full-time house-wife and mother. She had been trying for a long time to become pregnant, but with no success. Perhaps if they had a child, Tim would change. However, this hope was dashed when gynaecological tests revealed that she could never have children except by in vitro fertilisation. Tim and Caroline decided not to bother – or rather, he did. He said he felt they were probably happier as they were.

When Caroline again had irrefutable evidence of Tim's womanising, she confronted him. In another blazing row, Tim said it was hardly his fault if Caroline was so frigid and lacking in libido that he had no choice but to turn to other women. Caroline then decided that Tim's womanising must be her fault, and made up her mind to go for sex therapy. She had given up her job so as to be more available and 'sexy' for Tim when he got home from work, but it didn't seem to have had any effect on his behaviour.

PETER – THE SELF-MADE MAN

Peter was a truly nice guy, a doctor, dedicated to his patients. He was a GP, working both in the NHS and privately. Everybody wanted to get on to Peter's list – he never gave his patients the bare 10 minutes, but really tried to sort out their problems. He was also that increasingly rare creature, a doc-tor who didn't mind making home visits.

Not many people knew that Peter had come from a very poor background, and had a terrible struggle to qualify as a doctor. For most of Peter's life, his father was out of work, but Peter had pulled himself up by his bootstraps. As well as being so conscientious in his work as a doctor, he was on numerous committees, and involved in voluntary organisations. He was also married with two children, and had a house with a large garden.

Although his career was so important to him, Peter was racked with guilt about how little time he was able to spend with his wife and family. Maggie, his wife, suffered from M.E. (Myalgic encephalomyelitis) and was frequently confined to bed. Peter spared no effort in trying to find a cure or suitable treatment for Maggie, who was sometimes so tired by the effort of getting out of bed that she had to get straight back in. Never mind, he could cope.

Peter tried to be there for everybody, including his now aged parents. Everybody seemed to need him – Maggie, his children, who were still only eight and 10, and so often didn't really have a mother around, his patients, the charities he worked for. Where would it all end?

It was hardly surprising, perhaps, that Peter got into the habit of having two or three whiskies before he went to bed. The drinks helped him relax and get to sleep, for Peter suffered from insomnia.

DANIEL – THE CARING SON

At the age of 35, Daniel was still single, still living at home with his elderly mother. Much the youngest of six children, Daniel had been born when his mother was 45 and thought she would not have any more childrer. She had not wanted Daniel, but he became the most adored child of all, petted, spoilt, indulged. Daniel and his mother were always very close, especially as his father had never been much good – violent, abusive, a gambler. Daniel's mother turned to him for comfort and as a confidant. Daniel felt sorry for her, having such a hard lot in life, and vowed that she would never want for anything while he was around.

So he wrapped his life around her needs, getting a good job so that he could provide for her in her old age. They went on holiday together, and everybody said how lucky Mavis was to have such a wonderful son. At one time, Daniel had hoped to get married and have a family of his own, but now there was no chance – Mother came first.

Daniel worked his way up to manager of his local bank and his hobby was cookery. He loved to cook gourmet meals and gave dinner parties for his friends – and for his mother's friends. He was now considerably overweight, and getting fatter all the time. But food was his only pleasure – how could he deprive himself just to be slim? Better to be fat and happy.

CODEPENDENTS ALL

Five ordinary people, each of whom could easily be a character in a soap opera, with their ongoing problems. But what is wrong with them? Haven't they all had to cope with a lot of responsibility and shouldered it as well as could be expected? Where is the codependency, this condition which is now increasingly being recognised as an illness in its own right?

The answer is: *each of these people is doing their utmost to meet the needs of others, instead of living their own lives:*

- Susan has dedicated her life to being supportive to Richard, but who is being supportive to her?
- Penny cared for her mother, then her invalid husband – but who cared for her?
- Peter, the doctor, lives for his work and tries to meet all the needs of his patients and family – but who is meeting his needs?
- Caroline is gradually narrowing her life to the point where she is doing little else but trying to control Tim's womanising.
- Daniel has dedicated his life to looking after his mother – but who has dedicated themselves to Daniel?

In our present society, such people are frequently considered admirable ... giving up everything to look after others. They are seen as unselfish, altruistic and self-sacrificing. Most probably, they have all told themselves that they don't have any serious needs of their own, that their happiness comes from looking after others and tending to their needs. Yet the fact of the matter is that none of them is happy.

Susan is desperately trying to hang on to Richard, when she knows that the marriage is at an end and that nothing will stop him from leaving her. She long ago gave up her own promising career and is financially dependent. She is terrified that her status as a company director's wife will cease, and that she will have to eke out a miserable life on whatever handouts and maintenance she can wrest from him.

After a lifetime of looking after her mother and then her husband, Penny is now dependent upon tranquillisers. Otherwise, she becomes so depressed that she can't carry on her caring job.

Caroline is miserable because she feels she is undersexed, and that she has some deep-seated sex-related problem which has driven Tim to look for satisfaction in one-night stands.

Peter has started drinking, as a way of comforting himself after a day's work is finally done; and he feels exhausted most of the time.

Daniel has sacrificed hopes of marriage and his prospects are lessened as he overeats and becomes less and less attractive.

The non-codependents among us might ask: why do these people feel they have to minister so totally to the needs of others – especially when their caring is not making them feel happy and fulfilled? Why are they sabotaging their own lives and health for others, in most cases people who patently do not deserve or appreciate such sacrifices?

The answer here is: for some deep-seated reason, they feel driven and that they have no choice. Although at first all these people may seem exceptionally caring, loving and unselfish, if we look a little closer at the case histories we may be able to see a different side to their behaviour, a side that perhaps they themselves would find hard to acknowledge. Although they all appear to be pushed around and manipulated by those close to them, they are all actually trying to exert some kind of control over their loved ones. They are being compelled by a strong inner voice which says: 'If you are needed by others, they will never leave you.'

Above all, codependents equate *need* with *love*, so that they can feel loved only if they are deeply needed, only if it appears that the significant others in their lives could not possibly manage without them.

Peter wants to be in charge, to be seen as the ultimate coper and carer, the man who can take anything life may throw at him. He wants to be the all-powerful, all-commanding, all-respected doctor. To some extent, he has succeeded in this. His patients worship him. His wife relies on him. He is having to be both a mother and a father to his children. Yet at the same time, Peter is allowing all of these people to control him. He feels that he would be nothing without his status as a doctor, without having so very many people relying on him all the time. He wants to be a rock, unassailable, completely solid and reliable – yet inwardly he feels empty, at times suicidal, and in great danger of cracking up.

All her life, Susan has been playing a supportive, secondary role, content apparently to live in her husband's shadow. She has been living life at second hand, vicariously. Yet, at the same time, she sees herself as the one in control. She has persuaded herself that Richard's success is all down to her, and the greatest compliment anybody could pay her is: he owes it all to you. Many of her friends have actually said this, and Susan truly believes it. But why did this woman feel she had to put everything into her husband's career and nothing into her own? Why did she so readily give up any hope of being a professional pianist to follow him around the world? Susan has hardly touched a piano for over 30 years.

Why did Caroline give up her job to try and be a 'proper' wife to Tim, when it is obvious to all that he will be a womaniser whatever she does? Why does Daniel feel so strongly welded to his mother? Why did Penny actually choose to look after another invalid when she could have been free after her mother's death?

It may all seem incomprehensible, until we understand what a stranglehold the tentacles of codependency can have. Codependents, for various reasons, are powerless to run their own lives. They must always be at the beck and call of others. Having only a very hazy notion of who they are, it becomes easier to define themselves in terms of their roles, or relationships to other people, safer to allow the feelings and actions of others to rule their lives. Thus, Susan is the 'supportive wife', the 'devoted mother'; Daniel is the 'caring son'; Caroline is the 'wronged woman'. If you can identify with this tendency, understanding how and why they feel as they do can help you to deal with your own feelings of this kind.

ADDICTION TO OTHERS

One definition of codependency is that it is an addiction to an addict or some other person. A codependent 'uses' people in much the same way as a chemically dependent person will use alcohol or drugs. Codependents are the ultimate busybodies, wanting to be useful, wanting to be in charge, and, like other addicts, they need to achieve a high. They get a buzz from feeling useful, needed and wanted – and an almighty letdown when they sense they are not being appreciated enough, or that other people simply trample all over them. They put themselves out endlessly for others, and then wonder why people are so often ungrateful, so dismissive, so nasty.

The syndrome of codependency so frequently manifests itself around those with addictions, and because of this it was first noticed in addiction and detoxification centres. After all, who could be more needy than somebody in the grip of an uncontrollable addiction? It has been estimated, for instance, that somebody with an eating disorder – anorexia or bulimia – can keep up to 20 codependents busy. Those who suffer from an obvious addiction tend to attract codependents, people who will wrap their lives around them.

Very frequently, an alcoholic man will have a codependent wife, somebody who is always there to rescue him, to mop up after him, hide the drink, excuse his behaviour – even perhaps drink with him so that they can both be in the same boat. In the old days, as mentioned in the introduction, such spouses were known as 'enablers'. But the term came to be considered as extremely cruel and pejorative and now that the word 'codependent' has replaced it, the syndrome is at last being studied sympathetically. Blame does not now attach to these people who unwittingly collude in the addiction and enable it to continue.

Codependency is seen around drug-addicted teenagers,

who often have parents who do all they can to help their afflicted child. Such parents always take in the addict, pay his or her bills or bail, settle debts, provide food, clothing and shelter, and make them promise not to take drugs again. But the teenagers always do – and are enabled to continue because every time Mum and Dad rescue them from difficulties. When the teenagers get worse and worse, and possibly end up being hospitalised or in prison, the desperate parents ask themselves: where did we go wrong? Didn't we do everything we could?

What these parents don't usually realise is that they are exhibiting codependent behaviour. At the very heart of the codependent's problems is the deep-seated feeling that other people are aspects of yourself. You have to help Mum because, after all, you are part of her, she gave you life. You have to help your children, rescue them from danger even when they are grown up because they are yours and blood is thicker than water. And they didn't ask to be born, did they? If you are codependent you cannot detach yourself from the person you are codependent on, and in your fearfulness of losing them, or that bad things might happen to them, you *cling* and mistake this for love.

You have to help your husband or wife, because these people, too, are part of you. Didn't you agree to become 'one flesh' when you married? How can you separate yourself from the people you love, even when they behave terribly and let you down? If somebody close to you lets you down, it is like letting yourself down.

A codependent sincerely believes in all these obligations, all these reasonings, and they are encouraged by society. Most of us are brought up to consider the needs of others, to be unselfish, to help out. If we don't, we risk censure and the disapproval of those around us.

But, as this book will show, there is a vast difference between being ordinarily loving and caring, and having the best interests of family members at heart – and being codependent. In essence, a codependent person cannot ever see what might be best for others, because he or she has become incapable of detaching, and understanding clearly what the needs of others might be. They actually project their own needs onto other people. In a way, horrible though this may seem, they become like leeches, clinging on to those around them for their own sense of identity and status.

Codependents are always looking for a needy individual to latch on to. And with so many sad cases or 'lost causes' to embrace, they will always be successful. They are found in all walks of life, as doctors, nurses, therapists, social workers, loyal secretaries, dedicated workers, self-sacrificing parents, politicians, teachers, voluntary workers, compulsive over-achievers, and sometimes – yes – as active addicts. Codependency may be hidden under the anaesthetising influence of alcohol, drugs or gambling, but often when the sufferer achieves recovery from chemical dependency, an underlying codependence will be revealed.

We should add that the long list of jobs which tend to attract codependents should not be taken to mean that everybody in these fields is a sufferer from the syndrome, and is looking for love, status and identity through other people. But in all these professions, there is a danger that codependency will surface, masquerading as natural love and care. A person is likely to be a codependent if, whatever they do, the people in their care never seem to get better, or if they themselves are made miserable and ever unsatisfied by what they do.

As we have said, some codependents are compulsive over-achievers. Not all put their careers in abeyance to minister to the needs of others. But, even with the over-achievers, if you look closely, you will see that they are allowing other people to pull their strings. It's as if they have said to themselves: if I'm not careful, people might control me, so I'd better get in first and control them. Dictators, either of countries or as 'little Hitlers' in a tiny sphere – martinet headmasters, overbearing bosses, fiercely controlling husbands and fathers or wives and mothers, bullies of all kinds – are all codependents. You never know what *they* are really like, inside, because they make sure that nobody ever gets very close to them.

If you ask codependents how they are, you invariably get the answer: 'I'm all right.' They will never dwell on any problem, and even when their difficulties seem insuperable and you wonder how on earth they will manage, they will assure you that 'it's not so bad', or 'it's getting better' – although the situation is patently getting worse.

SIGNIFICANT OTHERS

A well-known American worker in the field of codependency, Sharon Wegscheider-Cruse, who herself suffered from the syndrome for many years, defines it as:

> *a specific condition characterised by preoccupation and extreme dependence on another person – emotionally, socially, sometimes physically.*
>
> *This dependence, nurtured over a long period of time, becomes a pathological condition that affects the codependent in all other relationships.*

Another definition of a codependent is somebody who might say, or at least think: without you, I'm nothing. It would be very hard to be codependent if alone on a desert island. A codependent needs people in the same way as an alcoholic needs a drink, or a gambler needs to place a bet.

Just pause to reconsider our five initial case histories (we want to stress that these are *ordinary* stories – we shall be discussing more devastating examples of codependency later in the book). Ask yourself where these people would be without the significant others in their lives. Where would Susan be without Richard? Where would her sense of identity come from? She is the archetypal wife and mother – Mrs Him. But who is she, once separated from her husband and children?

Penny identified herself as a 'carer', a looker-afterer *par excellence*. At an early age, she became Mother's Little Helper, the one who cleaned up the mess, hid the bottles, became responsible. Who would look after Mother if Penny didn't? Horror of horrors, the neighbours might find out about her drinking problem.

Peter, the high achiever, seems successful enough in his own right so how has he blotted out his own identity? He has identified himself so closely with his profession that it is impossible to think of him, or for him to think of himself, as anything but 'the doctor.' Take away that doctor label, and Peter's sense of status would immediately disappear.

Daniel is the perfect son, the son any mother would be proud to have. Caroline is the long-suffering wife of a flagrant Casanova, but who would she be without Tim's infidelities to give her a sense of being a blameless victim? She has identified herself as the wronged wife – and increasingly lives by that label.

The concept of codependency can be difficult to appreciate, especially as it is so intimately bound up with what society tells us is good and right. It is good to be a carer – the newspapers are always full of stories about carers who give up everything to look after aged relatives or handicapped children. It is good to be concerned, to be loyal, to be a conscientious worker.

But codependency is *inappropriate*, over-the-top loyalty, caring and supportiveness. Codependents work far beyond the call of duty, even when there is no need for it. Codependents are millionaires who must make the next million, men who must have a fifth wife, or who are never satisfied with one Rolls Royce. They can never have enough of whatever it is they crave – love, sex, money, fame, position – or even the reverse, being kicked into the gutter and trampled all over. Whatever you dish out to a codependent, they will come back for more. They are the wives who return again and again to a violent husband, telling themselves that this time he'll change, this time he really does mean it. Do you recognise any of these traits in yourself?

When a particular coping strategy does not seem to work, a codependent will redouble efforts, rather than trying to change the strategy. For instance, if an alcoholic finds the bottles that his codependent wife has hidden, she will immediately think that she must find a better hiding place – a completely ineffective strategy for overcoming somebody else's alcoholism.

If a violent husband hits his wife after he has promised not to, the wife will frequently believe that it's because she hasn't been nice enough to him, cooked him good enough meals, been sympathetic enough to his difficulties. In other words, the codependents tend to blame themselves for the addict's behaviour, and resolve to be more perfect, more watchful, more sexy or whatever, in future.

This of course, comes down again to control. The codependent is trying to control the actions of others by certain types of behaviour. The fact that these strategies never work makes the codependent feel even more miserable and lacking in self-esteem. If you can identify with these traits, perhaps this is how you are feeling right now.

An individual under the influence of codependency can never see that it is impossible to control another's behaviour – other than by putting them under lock and key.

Codependents again and again choose unrewarding people to marry or with whom to form long relationships. They never seem to learn their lesson. They will say that this is the way they are made, that they know they are fools for being taken for continuous rides, but they'll never change now.

At this stage you may ask: isn't codependency, then, simply being human? Surely all of us have fallen into this trap. Anybody who has ever been in love, for example, will have been profoundly affected by the other person's behaviour. Love poetry, from earliest times, is full of how devastated lovers are by the cruelty and inconsistency of the loved one. It's natural, surely, for parents to be upset when their children let them down, or for a wife to be angry and tearful when her husband is unfaithful, or announces that he's going to leave?

Yes, of course, all these feelings are natural. But the basis of codependency is not simply that we may be profoundly affected by the behaviour or feelings of other people, so much as that we cannot see other people as separate from ourselves, with their own set of behaviours, feelings and actions which we may not share. For a codependent, somebody else's actions are, essentially, *their* actions.

INFANTILE STATE

For non-codependents the experience of merging, becoming one with the beloved, lasts for only a short time, then separate identities reassert themselves as the relationship matures. Codependents, however, remain in this infantile state of wanting to merge with the other, and become part of them. Although they may be intelligent, sophisticated people, emotionally they tend to remain at this infantile dependent state. As we shall see later, certain kinds of parenting encourage infantile dependence, and foster codependency. A codependent has never grown up emotionally, and longs to regress to that childlike state of being one with Mummy. Up to the age of about two, children do not perceive other people as separate from themselves. Codependents are adults who can *never* see other people as separate – and that is at the heart of their relationship problems.

But as with anything else, there are degrees, and we are talking here about serious manifestations of the syndrome which eventually make the sufferer's life unliveable, unmanageable. Raging codependents are those who have let other people's behaviour and wishes affect them to such an extent that they have become empty shells, just waiting to be filled up by somebody else's character, desires and inclinations.

Codependents are happy when the significant others in their lives are happy, sad when they are sad, angry when they are angry. Their emotions are swayed this way and that, so that in the end, the codependent never knows what she or he really thinks or believes or feels. In fact, they cannot allow themselves to feel. They become mirrors for others, reflecting emotions and states of mind. At the same time, codependents are often extremely skilful in making other people feel guilty.

DENYING REALITY

Whenever you feel *compelled* to put other people first at the expense of yourself, you are denying your own reality, your own identity. Some people mistakenly imagine that it is Christian to put others first, but Christ asked his followers only to love others as themselves – not instead of themselves. You can never truly love another person unless you can first love yourself.

If you don't love yourself, people may need you, they may admire you, they may feel you're a wonderful coper – but they won't love you. In fact, non codependents often feel guilty because they can't love a codependent. This person is so nice, so self-sacrificing, so loyal – so why aren't they lovable? Because so often there is nothing to love – there is no essence, no self, readily accessible or on display to others.

One of the commonest remarks codependents make is: after all I've done for you, this is how you treat me. They have enormous expectations of others, expectations which are rarely met. They hope and pray that the other people in their lives will change and improve. Many sincerely believe that the world would be a far better place if only everybody would change their behaviour for the better. It never occurs to the codependent that *his or her* behaviour could do with modification or improvement.

Because other people never come up to scratch, in the codependent's eyes, he or she is always miserable, teetering on the edge of a crisis. Life never goes smoothly. They can be drama-queens, or kings, needing to put on a performance and be the centre of attention. And they never feel good about themselves. That, really, is the hallmark of a true codependent: somebody who is chronically miserable on the inside, however successful the outside may look. Could that description apply to you?

GLORIFYING THE SYNDROME

It's a sad fact that many of the most popular songs extol codependency as the right and proper way to relate to other people. We are indebted here to Dr Wayne Dyer, author of *Your Erroneous Zones*, one of the first books on codependency (although the term had not then been coined) for compiling a list of songs which glorify the syndrome. Here are some of the more codependent lines from these songs:

You make me feel brand new.
You make me feel so young.
You're the cream in my coffee, you're the salt in my stew. You will always be, My necessity, I'd be lost without you.
People who need people are the luckiest people in the world.
You are the sunshine of my life.

Non-codependent versions of these lines might go:

> *I make myself feel brand new.*
> *I make myself feel so young.*
> *I'm the cream in my coffee. I'm the salt in my stew. I will*
> *always be, My necessity, I'd be in exactly the same position as*
> *I am now (if not better) without you.*
> *People who need people are the most miserable, codependent*
> *people in the world.*
> *I am the sunshine of my life.*

As Dr Dyer points out, these lines are hardly going to send any song soaring to the top of the hit parade, but they express healthy, rather than unhealthy, sentiments. For codependents, however, the original lines spell out all the messages they love to hear – that you're nobody until somebody cares. Or notices. Because some codependents are not caring at all, but rebels, drop outs, criminals, even. These are the attention-grabbing codependents. Although at first, they may seem to be the opposite of the self-sacrificing, caring doormat-type codependent, in fact, they are screaming at other people to react to them. They are still nobody until somebody cares, somebody loves them.

We can very easily confuse codependency with love. Falling in love mimics severe codependency, when people 'fall in love' very often, and frequently they go through emotional turmoil because of yet another failed or unsatisfactory love affair. If we genuinely love, we will wish what is best for the other person, rather than wanting the beloved to modify his or her behaviour to suit our wishes.

True love involves detachment, being able to let go. Codependent love wishes to bind, strangle, cling. Parents who love their children will wish them well all their lives, but will not be hurt or disappointed when the children's lives do not conform to the parents' hopes or expectations. The codependent finds it difficult to appreciate that children are completely separate beings for whom they have taken on only temporary responsibility.

COMPOUNDING THE NEGATIVE

One patient who attended a codependency clinic confessed that her problems had become so bad that she immediately fell in love with anybody who smiled at her, or who had a kindly word.

The fact is that when one needy person falls in love with another needy person – another codependent or addict, perhaps – then neither can ever be satisfied or fulfilled. In time, the relationship, which may have seemed so exciting and all-consuming at first, turns into one of annoyance, resentment, jealousy and bitterness, even hate. When two people dominated by immature dependence on one another try to form a relationship, the two negatives don't make a positive, but merely compound the negativity.

The people in our case histories would probably tell you, and fervently believe, that they act as they do out of love. Susan genuinely believes she loves her husband; that's why she has followed him around. Caroline loves Tim, which is why she is trying to reform him. Penny loved her mother and her invalid husband Bill, which is why she had devoted her life to looking after them. Daniel loves his mother; no mother and son could be more close. Peter loves not only his family but all of his patients. He cares so much about them that he's prepared to risk his own health in looking after them.

Yet these people don't love – they need. If you really love somebody, you don't need them in this suffocating way. The beloved will always feel stifled, in a straitjacket, when he or she perceives such need. It may even bring out their sadistic side; they may enjoy seeing how far they can go before you crack. But codependents rarely crack – they just take more and more rubbish from other people. Don't let this happen to you.

If we are describing the situation you find yourself in, don't despair! Recovery is possible and this book is designed to help you find a way out and live your life in a more fulfilled way. Indeed, if you can identify yourself as codependent then you have already taken the first step towards recovery and begun the process of dismantling the denial which has entrapped you.

LIVING THROUGH OTHERS

A marvellously acute example of a codependent is Beattie in the British Telecom television advertisements. Beattie (superbly played by Maureen Lipman) is portrayed as the archetypal Jewish mother, completely dependent on her husband, sons, daughters, grandchildren. She needs to be needed – and always suspects that they don't think as much of her as she does of them. Beattie is always ready to see the negative, uncaring side of things. When she first sees a fax machine, she remarks that now there will be *two* ways she won't be receiving messages from her family. Beattie seems amusing because we all know people like her. Jewish or not – eternal complainers, always trying to make people feel guilty, gaining their entire identity from the other people in their lives.

The famous 'ology' ad, where Beattie listens to the news that her grandson has failed all his exams, exemplifies Beattie's reliance on other people to bring her status. The only reason she wants Daniel to have an 'ology' is so that she can be a proud grandmother. People like Beattie, in real life, are those who exact huge amounts of emotional blackmail. They are are full of self-pity, and can be devasted for days if one of their children doesn't ring after having faithfully promised. Such people want to control every second of their family's lives, even when the family members have long grown up and should have gone their own ways. Beattie spends her time trying to control other people and, in turn, is controlled by them. No wonder she is up and down emotionally all the time, never stable for a minute.

It's easy for those who are not troubled by codependency to say: if these other people are bothering you so much, making your life such a misery, why don't you just forget about them, and live your own life? Well – if you could, you would, and that's where the basic problem lies. Asking any codependent to give up people is like asking a nicotine addict to give up smoking, or an alcoholic to give up drink.

If they could, they would. The point is, their behaviour is compulsive, and until they can recognise the nature of their relationships, they will have no choice of how to behave. To complicate the situation further, such people will usually vehemently defend themselves, in order to maintain the charade and prevent the painful truth from seeping into their consciousness.

Codependents are fearful people and they frequently use the burdens they have brought upon themselves as an alibi for not developing their own resources or talents. Perhaps you have done the same? Of course Penny cannot hope to live her own life or fulfil her own potential – she has to look after Mother. Of course Daniel cannot get married and move into his own house – he too has Mother to consider. Of course Susan could never become a professional pianist – she had to see to Richard's needs.

Codependents always have a ready-made alibi for not doing what, in some ways, they wished they had. If they never try, or put themselves on the line, they can never fail. And how much better if, by caring for others they can gain admiration at the same time as never risking personal failure or rejection, or facing the fear which binds them.

Codependency can affect men and women equally, although its more obvious manifestations are frequently found in women. One reason for this is because in our society women are encouraged to become the carers, to put their own needs and talents on hold to become secondary and supportive. If you ask where are all the great women composers, poets and artists, the answer is: they were very often married to the great male composers, poets and artists! Mozart's sister, for instance, was equally talented in her youth. But women often give it up to care for the 'real' genius – the man. Many men of genius have found codependent women extremely useful. One of the aspects hindering recovery is that codependents are so useful to the other people in their lives, that these others don't want the codependent to recover, and may actively sabotage such attempts. So many people, particularly men, have been rendered so helpless by the codependents in their lives that they live in terror of having to manage on their own.

Perhaps the worst, most sinister aspect of codependency, and the one which forms the heart of this book, is that it is passed from generation to generation, in the guise of normal behaviour. A child who grows up in a codependent household believes that this kind of behaviour is normal and, knowing nothing else, simply repeats it.

CAUSE AND EFFECT

The reason we know that codependency is unhealthy is because it brings about so much chronic illness. The most common consequence of codependency is depression, very often severe. Another frequent consequence is active addiction, whether to alcohol, shopping, food, gambling or prescribed or street drugs. It has even been claimed by some researchers in America that codependency can also lead to cancer, heart disease, lowered immunity and resistance to infections, M.E. and anorexia.

The reason why it can bring about so much illness is that it is a stressful state. Codependents always feel nervous inside. They have little self-confidence and almost no sense of identity. They are frantic worriers, take excessive responsibility for others, and can never relax.

Research has established that people who suffer from severe codependency are rarely, if ever, really well. They are always going to the doctor with mysterious, undiagnosable complaints, and never seem to get better, whatever treatment is tried. They may confess to the doctor that they would be all right if only their responsibilities didn't weigh so heavily upon them.

Work on codependency and the related subject of addiction remains controversial and is by no means accepted by all psychiatrists, psychologist and doctors. There are still very few centres in the UK where people can be treated for codependency, and many doctors will still not have heard of the term. But many people whose problems have remained a mystery for years, can be successfully treated at last, once they understand the impact of codependency, and can relate it to certain events and behaviours in their own home.

The origins of codependency are examined in more detail in the next chapter.

2 ‖ How codependency starts

Codependency, as we have seen, is the predominance in one's personality of an infantile reliance on other people for one's own sense of identity. But how does it start?

The explanations we give in this chapter are complex because our lives are often complex. And no level of our being can be taken in isolation. Let's look at the various aspects of our lives:

- We first live as individuals, each with a certain genetic disposition and mental structures.
- We also live as part of a family, with different relationships within that family. (We may experience more satisfactory relationships with some than with others.)
- We live in a society which exerts pressure upon the family.
- We live as part of humankind. Here, there are factors that are common to all societies.

During our lifetimes we progress from birth to old age, and at every stage in our development there are different tasks to be negotiated:

- Our first task is to establish trust.
- In adolescence the peer group becomes important, and sexual relationships are negotiated.
- In early adulthood we become interested in careers and maybe in forming a family.

- In mid-life we begin to evaluate what has been achieved so far.
- In old age we mellow and gain perspective and wisdom.

How we negotiate these tasks is affected by how they were negotiated by our parents, our grandparents and their parents before them. It is important to realise that each person exists and develops within a much larger framework. Understanding one's make-up is rather like dismantling the different layers of a Russian doll!

In this chapter, therefore, we seek to offer explanations for codependency at each level, and to show the connections between them.

DYSFUNCTIONAL HOMES

American research has found that the syndrome develops during childhood and is liable to flourish in particular kinds of homes, such as those where either or both parents are alcoholics or otherwise chemically dependent. They are known as dysfunctional homes.

Because of their addiction, the adult(s) in the house cannot be properly 'there' for the children or the spouse. An alcoholic or addict is a sick person, so it is extremely difficult for him or her to be a good enough parent or partner – that is, one who can be consistent or reliable for their partner or the children. Chemical dependency means that all other aspects of life, including care giving and nurturing, take a secondary role. What nurturing and care giving is available tends to be erratic and unpredictable, and living in such a household becomes a precarious and anxiety-laden existence, dictated by the ups and downs, the highs and lows, the presence and absence of addictive behaviour.

Some alcoholic or addicted parents, however, may be extremely conscientious about providing enough clothes and food, warmth and shelter, and are not necessarily obviously neglectful parents. Indeed, some children from chemically dependent homes have 'everything' – an expensive education, music lessons, bikes, holidays abroad – that is, all the material things. But a chemically dependent parent will not be consistently there *emotionally* for the child – because of the dependency.

ROBERTA'S STORY

Roberta, a patient at the Codependency Clinic at St Joseph's, described her earliest memories thus:

> As a four-year-old I used to wake up and rush into Mummy's bedroom. She always slept with a glass of "water" beside her. Her hand would tremble as she reached for the glass, and I would notice beads of sweat on her forehead. She would grunt at me to go away. A little while later, Mummy would be up and about. She would make me my breakfast and make herself a glass of "lemonade". By lunchtime she was cheerful and would play with me. She would tell me she loved me, but she was very intense and sometimes would cry. I knew that meant she was tired and I would go and play by myself.
> 'I remember one day bringing her a model boat I had made, and telling her I loved her. She was so happy that she promised to buy me a big bar of chocolate. I was excited, but then she just fell asleep on the floor. (Sometimes when this happened I thought she was dead.) When Daddy came home, he behaved as he usually did – he stepped over her and pretended she wasn't there. He made me my tea and got me ready for bed. As I was about to go to bed, Mummy woke up and I ran to her and said "Mummy, Mummy, when can we go and get the chocolate?". She hit me in the face and told me I was a selfish slut. (I didn't realise then that she had suffered memory blackout.) Daddy pulled me away. I felt shocked and frozen inside. Daddy cuddled me and I noticed that he, too, was crying and upset. He told me that Mummy gets very tired and doesn't mean to be bad to me. I remember lying in my bed, trying to go to sleep. I was trying to understand what I had done wrong for my mother to be so cross, and I wanted to know how I could make her happy again so I could get my bar of chocolate.

In this example, the variability in maternal behaviour caused Roberta to seek to get her needs met by mastering or controlling the behaviour of her mother. No wonder she became confused as to what is real and what is not real in her later life.

COVER-UP AND DENIAL

Many homes where there is chemical dependency will be obviously neglectful and abusive, but this is by no means always the case. It may not be spotted, because family members will all have vested interests in making sure outsiders don't know what really goes on – or how painful the situation is. And the aspect, above all else, which causes the problem of codependency is denial that there is anything wrong, denial that the children have anything but a loving and nurturing home, denial that the parents are anything but perfect.

You can have a chemically dependent home where the children escape codependency. But nobody can escape where there is denial of some form of human misery – even in teetotal, fundamentalist Christian homes where all self-indulgences such as alcohol, gambling and smoking are absent.

COMMONPLACE ADDICTION PROBLEMS

For years, it was thought that addiction among adults bad enough to cause serious disruption in the home was relatively rare. And as for denial and pretence – well, that seemed a ridiculous concept. But now, thanks to investigation and research, we know that alcohol dependency and other kinds of addiction are very common, and the ramifications may affect families even when three or four generations removed.

It is estimated that one in four homes in America houses an alcoholic, and that at least one of a child's eight great-grandparents will most probably have had an alcohol or other addiction problem, with alcohol being the most common, simply because for centuries it has been the most easily available mood-altering drug. In Britain and Europe, the devastating effects of alcohol and other addictions on families and children is only just beginning to be realised.

It was thought until recently that the worst danger for children from alcoholic homes was foetal alcohol syndrome, which causes physical and mental handicap from the mother drinking during pregnancy. The only other danger was thought to be the violence which may come from having an alcoholic father. We are only just beginning to appreciate that all adult chemical dependencies can have far-reaching effects on children which may not be obvious at first.

Apart from the presence, or otherwise, of chemical dependency, there will always be at least two significant factors in homes which breed codependents: the parents will, in important ways, either emotionally, or physically, not be properly there for the children. The children, though, will be there for the sake of the adults. Whenever a child wins some prize or passes an important exam, the parent will take some of the credit.

A typically codependent remark crops up in D. H. Lawrence's *Sons and Lovers*, where Paul Morel's mother exclaims, when he wins a painting competition: 'I knew we should do it!' This famous novel tells the story of a typically codependent home – the father is not there emotionally, is often drunk, and so the mother makes mini-husbands of her sons, thus stopping them from ever being able to make proper relationships of their own.

Non-alcoholic ways in which parents may not be 'there' for the children can include:

• violence and sexual abuse
• workaholism
• gambling
• tranquilliser addiction
• womanising
• chronic invalidism
• frequent journeys abroad
• death
• suicide
• being unemployed or unemployable
• frequent hospitalisation

- mental or physical handicap
- excessive religiosity
- rigid rules and regulations
- homes where children are never allowed to be themselves, but must always be pleasing the adults.

SHAME-BASED FAMILIES

The kind of home which tends to favour the development of codependent attitudes is one where there is enormous pretence, rather than any acknowledgement of painful realities. Such homes are known as shame-based family systems. In fact, the concept of shame is central to understanding codependency. Because there is a deep sense of shame, either about an addiction, or about the behaviour of a family member – or, because one or both parents came from such a home themselves – enormous efforts are usually made to pretend that everything is normal, and that this is an exceptionally happy and close-knit family. Only the family members know what is going on, and very often they won't admit it, even to themselves. So there is always an ongoing cover up, which prevents family members having a strong sense of personal identity. How can you learn to be yourself when you have had to play a false part from your earliest years?

There is a further, more complex way that shame operates to cause dysfunction. D. H. Lawrence, who perhaps more than any other author of modern times understood the origins of the feelings we now know as codependent, expresses it succinctly in his novel *The Rainbow* (1915):

Then suddenly, perhaps the next day, her soul would almost start out of her body as her father turned on her, shouting: 'Who has been dancing and trampling across where I have just sown seeds? I know it's you, nuisance. Can you find nowhere else to walk, but just over my seedbeds? But it's like you to have no heed but to follow your own greedy nose.' It had shocked him in his intent world to see the zig-zagging lines of deep little footprints across his world.

The child was infinitely more shocked. Her vulnerable little soul was flayed and trampled. Why were the footprints there? She had not wanted to make them. She stood dazzled with pain and shame and unreality. Her soul, her consciousness seemed to die away. She became shut off and senseless, a little creature whose soul had gone hard and unresponsive. The sense of her own unreality hardened her like a frost, and the sight of her face, sharp and superior with self-asserting indifference made a flame of rage go over him. He wanted to break her.

'I'll break your obstinate little face,' he said through shut teeth, lifting his head. The child did not alter in the least. The look of indifference, complete glancing indifference, as if nothing but herself existed to her, remained fixed.

Yet far away, in her, the sobs were tearing her soul. And when he had gone she would go and creep under the parlour sofa and lie clunched in the silent hidden misery of childhood. And when she crawled out after an hour or so, she went rather stiffly to play. She wished to forget, she cut off her childish soul from memory, so that the pain and the insult should not be real.

This passage illustrates brilliantly how shame can function to cut off and send into hiding the very essence of a child's being. The child, in order to protect itself from the threat of annihilation, retreats inwards and destroys the interpersonal bridge so that further pain and damage cannot be inflicted. Once hidden and submerged, the 'inner child' is protected and safe, and a stiff, defiant, angry or submissive front is established. The process of recovery from codependency involves the *rediscovery* of the 'child within' who was long ago shamed into hiding, and it requires building once again the interpersonal bridge which can bring nourishment and love. However, this is not an easy task and much psychological work must be accomplished before it is possible. There are no easy fences or comfortable ways to achieve this goal.

PERSONAL RESPONSIBILITY

We must stress again here, as we have elsewhere, that describing the origins of codependency is not the same as blaming the parents. Obviously, if the parents could have done better, they would have. They did the best they could, given their own pain.

In one case that came to St Joseph's Centre, staff members managed to trace the origin of codependency back through several generations, to about 1840. It probably went even further back than that, so dishing out blame is a futile exercise. Also, once you've stopped blaming – if ever you can stop – the situation remains the same. Recovery lies in being able to forgive parents, and stopping the rot by being able to admit denial of real feelings, and take personal responsibility for them.

The Churches' Council on Alcohol and Drugs, which puts addiction and alcoholism into a 'sin' concept, says:

> Sin starts in a small way, then grows, spreads and multiplies. It passes from parent to child, from friend to friend, from nation to nation. It becomes a habit, a way of life, rooted deeply within us . . . Addiction is a disease which limits freedom of will; a disease which affects not only the addict, but spreads to other members of the family, from generation to generation; a disease which affects whole societies.

If we substitute the less loaded term 'dysfunction' for 'sin', then we have a very useful definition of how these problems become increasingly enlarged.

Homes where there is obvious chaos, disintegration and violence, in some ways, may be *less* dysfunctional than outwardly 'respectable' middle class homes. With the obviously horrendous home it is more difficult to deny the reality, and the chances are greater that one family member will get into trouble bad enough to require therapy. Then, the whole family may be able to recover.

However, there are very many codependent and dysfunctional homes in stockbroker belt Surrey, very many with tennis courts, swimming pools and three cars on the curving drive. There may be maid's quarters and nannies or au pairs and children at expensive schools. Codependency is no respector of class or status. Much easier then, to put on a front.

This does not mean, of course, that every well-appointed home is a hotbed of codependency. But as a general rule, when somebody asserts that their home was perfect, their parents were perfect and that there were no problems of any kind in their childhood, codependency should be suspected. All homes have problems; healthy ones admit them, codependent homes keep them under wraps. The reason for this is clear – the hope is that if the problems are never brought to the surface, they will simply go away. In fact, the opposite happens – they fester and get progressively worse.

When problems are denied the fears and shame become submerged and repressed. They remain below conscious level and are liable to surface in inappropriate ways. Anorexic teenagers almost always come from codependent homes, as do teenage drug addicts, rebels and drop-outs. The television film *Cathy*, the true life story of a girl who died of anorexia at the age of 23, showed people beset with difficulties and problems, although desperately maintaining the appearance of a happy, well-adjusted family.

ALISON'S STORY

Shame functions alongside repression in codependent households. Here is a simple example of how shame can be repressed and internalised. Alison, an only child, who had been the centre of attention for very many years, felt jealous when a new baby was born. Her parents had wanted a new baby for a long time, and for them it was a joyous event. A notice went into the paper, saying that a new brother had arrived 'for Alison'.

Alison felt there must be something wrong with her when a jealous thought came into her mind. She could not tell anybody about her feelings, as she was supposed to love her new little brother so much. (In fact, it is a perfectly normal reaction for an existing child to feel jealousy when there is a new arrival – and sensitive parents will accept this and deal with it as a natural occurrence.)

However, Alison not only felt guilt at her jealousy, but as if her whole being was wrong. If she admitted, even to herself, that she was jealous, this would destroy the family 'myth' that this new birth was an unmitigatedly happy event. Because Alison felt desperately ashamed of herself for hating her baby brother, she buried this by taking responsibility for looking after him. In later life, she would tell people that she always had a very close relationship with her much younger brother and loved to take him out in his pram.

Because she never spoke about her guilt and shame, it became buried and Alison forgot about it. She married and had a child of her own. But soon after the baby was born, something nudged a deep repressed memory, and Alison began to drink. Eventually she was referred to an addiction centre for treatment and, thanks to expert therapy, her long-buried memories came to the surface.

During childhood and puberty, Alison had also tried to repress the knowledge that her parents actually preferred her brother – he was the long-awaited son, and they doted on him. But the myth in the family was that they were loved equally, and that there was no favouritism.

NARCISSISTIC ATTACHMENT

In codependent homes, parents are unable to see the children, however old they may be, as separate entities. This is known as a *narcissistic attachment*, meaning that the parent has great difficulty understanding what the child may be wanting. The child always exists for the parents' benefit, rather than as an individual human being. An unhealthily close relationship therefore grows up, one from which neither parent nor child can ever really break away.

Very many instances of daughters or sons being 'close' to mothers are examples of codependency, where the mother has poured out all her troubles to the child, as if he or she was a friend of the same age. This is inappropriate behaviour, but parents in pain are so preoccupied with their own troubles that they cannot appreciate what effect such confidences might have on their children. Such parents may regard themselves as self-sacrificing, giving up everything for the sake of the children – yet if, for example, a mother makes a confidant of her daughter, telling her all about the bad behaviour of her father, how is the daughter ever to have a proper relationship with her father? There will be fear and shame – the two emotions which are central to codependency.

In healthy families, the children will develop a sense of self-sufficiency and be happy to live away from home when they grow up – and the parents will be content that they have done their job. There will be contact, but this will be as between adults, with no guilt, emotional blackmail or recriminations on either side. In codependent homes by contrast, children never break away properly; because they have always had to exist in relation to the parents, they have never developed independence.

A related aspect of narcissistic attachment is how aggressive impulses in young children are viewed by their parents. From birth, these aggressive impulses of the child are misunderstood.

THE PARENTS' RESPONSE

The parent is not acting in bad faith, but is likely to have an idealised, unrealistic notion of what the child actually is. The expectation will be of a dear little baby, who coos and laughs and loves to be cuddled, and the codependent parent will usually have plenty of love and attention ready to lavish upon the child.

But when faced with aspects of the baby which are expressed aggressively and which may not be so lovable – screams for attention, soiled nappies, crying throughout the night and depriving the adults of sleep – there is often shock, and it can be very hard to cope. Under stress, parents then tend to fall back on their own basic resources, and their own experiences of being parented. Although these may not be consciously remembered, they will rise up to deal with adverse situations.

If only one parent is codependent then the other may be able to cope and offer support. But if both parents are codependent, then they are likely to turn on and blame each other as the child's needs threaten to overwhelm them.

The codependent parent will respond to the child in one of two characteristic ways.

- Either they will devise completely rigid behavioural strategies to regulate and control the child's demands, so that these cause minimal disruption and annoyance to the parents.
- Or they will go to the opposite extreme and give in to the child's every whim.

In the first instance, the child will be brought up 'by the book', with rigidly regulated feeding and bed times, for example. Usually, this kind of parenting is heavily rationalised by the parents who make such remarks as: 'He has to learn who's boss'; or, 'let him scream – if you keep picking him up he will only become spoilt.' Such parents will not admit, even to themselves, that they are rigidly controlling because of their own frustration, but will argue that it is all for the child's own good. These parents usually do not realise that the origins of this kind of behaviour comes from the kind of parenting they themselves have received.

People who have themselves been subjected to rigid parenting cannot admit that their parents may have been wrong, less than perfect. Their wish is to idealise their own parents because they wish to continue the illusion of the happy family. They want to see their own homes as being above criticism, and believe that they had the kind of parents who did what was best for their children. Because of this wish to idealise the parents, the behaviour is repeated.

In reality, parents who behave like this are not meeting the needs of their own children, but continuing to serve the needs of their own parents to be above reproach – and to keep safe the family secret of fear and shame.

In the other typically codependent response to children, the parents go to the opposite extreme and adopt a policy of letting the baby have everything he wants at the moment he wants it. The whole household is turned upside down to accommodate the baby, and the parents will very likely have read every book they can get on child development and proper parenting.

However, under the guise of meeting their child's every need, they deny their own as parents. This has the effect – usually hotly denied – of hostility towards the child who exerts such power. As the hostility towards the child grows, it will be repressed, and efforts redoubled to give the child everything, to love him, and deny him nothing.

When a child becomes the absolute centre of his parents' universe, he tends to grow up without a proper sense of separate identity. He may become hyperactive and unmanageable or exhibit other behavioural problems. Parents who treat their children as if they were their whole lives have the opposite attitude to their own rigidly controlling parents. Instead of trying to idealise their own parents, they will blame them for all the mistakes that have occurred, and vow never to repeat them with their own children.

What happens here is that the children become instruments of revenge, instead of being allowed to exist in their own right, and be themselves. In both cases, the child's development becomes skewed as it tries to comply to the parents' needs.

THE CHILD'S RESPONSE

Because the child is not allowed to be himself – in all his imperfections – he submerges his true feelings and tries to be what the parents want, in order to gain affection, or at least to gain attention.

The parents must be proved right, and their child rearing practices vindicated, so the child has to demonstrate that their methods are correct, and be happy and well adjusted. A sad, tearful child is a continual reproach. The child will also have to achieve what the parents would like to have achieved for themselves, and bring its parents credit and esteem. If this is not forthcoming, then there is something wrong with the child – who has had 'everything'.

The end result of either type of upbringing is that the codependency is passed on to the next generation, with greater risk that chemical dependency, eating disorders, depression, psychosomatic disorders, delinquency or drug addiction will arise in the child.

An overwhelming feature of all codependents is that they have reservoirs of rage, childish anger which was never allowed to come to the surface when they were small children. But because they feel so desperately ashamed of having all this anger inside them, they never allow it to show.

The most usual way of dealing with this anger is to pretend that it's not there, which is where *denial* starts. The typically codependent way of dealing with such anger is to become a caretaker, a giver. As the child has grown up having to deny needs from an early age, so the pattern continues into adulthood.

But the fact is that all humans do have needs, and we now understand that it is not healthy to deny one's own needs. If we persist in denial, as time goes on, the yawning emptiness grows, until it becomes unbearable and the codependent may resort to drugs, drink, or some other avenue of expression.

RELATED DISORDERS

We do not know for sure why some codependents develop related disorders and others don't. It is now known that for around 70 per cent of alcoholics, there is a likely genetic component, something in the brain which interacts with alcohol to predispose to alcoholism. But for the other 30 per cent, there seems to be no such component. All alcoholics, though, drink to oblivion. It would seem likely therefore that they are trying to medicate some deep seated pain.

DEVELOPING DEPENDENCY

This is how codependency can develop in a family where one member – let's say the father, as this is the most common pattern – is addicted to alcohol, gambling, womanising or work. Typically in such a household, the mother will be a codependent, having possibly herself come from a chemically-dependent background, which is why she has chosen an addict for a husband.

We may pause to ask here: if she has come from such a bad background, surely she has been able to see what it's like? Why can't she resolve not to repeat the pattern, and marry somebody without such problems? One reason is because, to somebody from this kind of home, alcoholics and addicts are normal, possibly all they have known. It can be difficult to avoid repeating a pattern when you have never known anything else.

More importantly, any child growing up in an addicted home will be very used to not having their needs met, which usually has the effect of making them feel they are wrong to have needs, rather than that the parents were unable to meet them. If the parents didn't meet them, surely they should not have existed?

Because of the great shame attached to this process, people from addicted households are terrified that somebody will find out what they are really like inside. The only type of person they can be certain won't do this is another addict – because no addict is ever 100 per cent 'there' for anybody else. So, in this sense, the addict is a 'safe' partner. He will need looking after, rescuing, and will never guess what a horrible person his wife really is, especially if she covers this up with love and care and rescue work.

In a typically codependent home, nobody must ever know that Dad has problems with drink. A codependent wife will dedicate herself to wrapping her life around her husband, trying to pretend that he is a good and proper father. Because this is what she wants to believe, this is the image she will try to instil into the children.

Children may come home to find Dad slumped in an armchair. 'What's the matter with Dad?' they may ask. 'Ssh,' says Mum, 'he's very tired. He's had a very heavy week at work.' The reality is, of course, that Dad is drunk. The children will be quite aware that Dad is drunk or, at the least, that there exists a family secret so shameful that it must never be mentioned. The whole family thus maintains the pretence that this home is happy, well-adjusted, normal.

But clearly, a life of pretence punctuated by bouts of alcoholism, rows, frequent absences, sexual or other abuse, will not be a very comfortable or secure place for children. They will grow up believing that, in some way, they have caused the problems.

SEXUAL ABUSE

It is very common for victims of sexual abuse, a not-infrequent occurrence in dysfunctional or chemically dependent homes, to believe that they are to blame, for having seduced or provoked the abuser.

A child who has been sexually abused and has internalised the abuse to the point where she is certain it is her fault, is not going to feel very good about herself as an adult. One outstanding feature of abused children is that they have no early memories – consciously they have completely forgotten what happened.

A parent may well turn to the child for sexual comfort when the partner is not 'there', either because of codependency or actual addiction. Also, a child is less likely to be judgmental. A child is safer than an adult, and will usually keep the secret of sexual abuse.

MOULDING BEHAVIOUR

Children growing up in dysfunctional homes are so sure that they are to blame for everything that they try to mould their behaviour to fit in with the prevailing pretence. Research has established that they are likely to do this in a number of ways:

- They may become the caretakers of their families, the 'heroes' who, by their great achievements, will show to the outside world that the family couldn't have been so bad.

  The 'heroes' become compulsive achievers, gain jobs of high status, and outwardly may appear very successful and content. It is the compulsiveness of the achieving which gives the game away. Anybody who can never stop achieving, who takes on an ever greater workload even when there is no need at all for this, is probably exhibiting codependency.

- Another common pattern is to become a 'lost child', saying: it's nothing to do with me. Such children vanish to their rooms and read or play records and simply do not join in with the rest of the family. They dissociate themselves from the chaos downstairs. The effect of this in later life is that they are unable to form close relationships, and never become involved any more than they can help.

- Very often in a dysfunctional family there will be a mascot – somebody who is always playing the clown, or acting cute. The child does this to deflect from the parent's problems, and take them, in a way, upon himself.
- A child may become a scapegoat, a rebel. Such children may become drug addicts, play truant from school, or, if girls, become pregnant at an early age, and appear uncontrollable. Sadly, there is no point, no logic in this action. They simply sabotage themselves and their chances in life.
- Other children become bullies, grandiose, turn to the bottle at an early age, or become Casanovas or nymphomaniacs.

It is probably safe to assume that most kinds of self-destructive behaviour have their roots in a dysfunctional family background.

It is perhaps becoming clearer now why codependents feel they must dedicate their lives to trying to meet other people's needs, expectations or worst fears. You may, for one reason or another, have such feelings yourself. It all starts when in childhood; your own deepest needs are continually not met to the point where you feel it must be terribly wrong to have any needs at all.

This is what St Joseph's believes are the origins of codependency. But this definition is not accepted by mainstream psychiatrists who, on the whole, do not take on board the full impact of addictive and chemically dependent behaviour on the whole family system.

CHARACTERISTICS OF CODEPENDENTS

All the symptoms that characterise codependency start early in life. But as they are not appropriate or healthy ways to be an adult, if they are not recognised and treated they will cause mental, physical and emotional problems as the years go by.

There is always this underlying feeling of discomfort, which never goes away, however much you attempt to anaesthetise or medicate it.

Hollow inside

Hilary Henriques is a worker at St Joseph's who has studied codependency at residential centres in America, and who has identified herself as a codependent, says:

> A typical codependent will often seem to the outside world to have a very good family relationship, even an enviable one. But he or she is actually brought up in pretence, so that they don't know what the truth is.
>
> Basically, we don't want to believe that the people we love are not all they might be. So we go to great lengths not to acknowledge their problems. As children, this denial is a form of survival, as it helps you to cope. The problem is that if you come from a family where there are enormous problems, you just never feel right inside.
>
> In a dysfunctional home, the children exist for the parents, rather than the other way round. A mother who has an abusive or alcoholic husband will often make a confidant of her child, giving the child completely inappropriate information. Because the mother is so wrapped up in her pain, she never stops to consider whether it might be good for the child to hear such stuff.
>
> In such families, the children become pawns, and assume an adult sense of responsibility. They are the children who seem grave or wise beyond their years.
>
> But as they have never had a proper childhood, they never really grow up.
>
> Parents who themselves have never had a proper childhood find it difficult to grow up. They may talk in baby voices or plead with somebody to take care of them. An alcoholic is crying out: take care of me. The codependent is only too ready to oblige, but at the same time feels desolate because there is nobody to care for her.

Outside appearance

Because so much has always depended on appearance, codependents are often extremely careful about how they look. They may well have harmonious-seeming homes, interior designed or colour-co-ordinated, and they are very clean and tidy. They concentrate on making the outside look as normal as possible in the vain hope that the inside will normalise itself as well. Yet it never does.

Tranquillisers

It's also extremely common for codependents to be addicted to tranquillisers, as they will often have been given these pills for anxiety or depression.

Settling for less

Another common characteristic is that they tend to sabotage themselves. Although one aspect of the disease is compulsive over-achievement, much more common is the one who settles for something less than could be achieved.

Fear of rejection

Because codependents are so terrified of rejection and abandonment – associated with their needs not being met as small children – they tend to take jobs and form relationships where rejection will not be an issue. Their feelings of self-worth are so low that they are certain they will be rejected before long, so they tend not to stay in jobs, or take jobs at less than their true abilities.

When it comes to forming relationships, or falling in love, they often end the affair first, before the other person has a chance to reject them. Whatever they do, there is no inner core of confidence, so they will easily give up, retreat into safety, relinquish their careers. Typical codependents are women who 'give up everything' to look after children and a home, secure in the knowledge that society will not condemn them for what appears to be their own decision.

Fear of failure

Although many women undoubtedly do gain great satisfaction and pleasure from bringing up a family and running a home, many others are doing this job because they are terrified of pitting themselves in the outside world, a dangerous place where they might be judged. How much safer to retreat into the family and home. Then there is always a convenient excuse for never having fulfilled early potential.

Of course, there are very many other reasons why many women do not achieve their personal potential. But, as we have said earlier, codependency is very much encouraged in women.

It's not so easy in our society for a male codependent to give up everything and look after a family and home, but the syndrome still manifests itself in similar ways. There are many men who have taken and kept jobs at what appears to be way below their true capacity. They may take 'safe' jobs, and rationalise this by saying they have to provide for their families, and this was why they could not be an actor, or writer, or other career they may have fancied at one time. Again, nobody will condemn them for this. Indeed, this is one aspect of codependent behaviour that is very commonplace.

Low self-esteem

They also have a diminished capacity to initiate or participate in loving relationships, because deep down they feel they are unlovable. As was pointed out earlier, they often (unconsciously) deliberately choose a partner who cannot be fully there for them. Codependents' parents never really loved them, because they themselves were incapable of proper love. So such people settle for less than the best, and often very little.

All the feelings of low self-worth and low self-esteem, the perception that one is not worth anything unless helping somebody even more needy, is at the heart of codependency.

Very often, addicts, abusers and other addicted people appear to others to be self-obsessed, selfish, demanding, childish, irresponsible. Their partners, by contrast, can appear generous, good-hearted, concerned, saintly and perfect.

Many codependents have excellent personal qualities and are extremely nice people, not just on the surface but all the way through. But deep inside themselves, they can't believe it.

LOOKING AGAIN AT OUR FIVE EXAMPLES

Let us return briefly to the five case histories outlined in Chapter 1. Eventually, all five sought treatment – not necessarily for codependency, but because their marriages were breaking up, because they suffered from depression, because in one way or another they felt they could not go on. All had suffered deprivation of one sort or another in childhood.

Susan

Susan, the wife who gave up everything to support her husband's career, had an abysmal childhood. Her father was a professional man who earned a lot of money as a lawyer, yet the family were never as well off as they should have been. There were two main reasons for this:

- All his life, her father kept a separate flat in another part of the town, and diaries which came into Susan's possession after his death revealed that he had been a secret opium and ether user.
- Also, Susan's mother became severely schizophrenic and had to be hospitalised after Susan's brother died at the age of 18. Because her father was never there, Susan fantasised him being the perfect father and herself as a wonderful, special child. As she had grown up with so little sense of her own identity, it became relatively easy for her to put all her energies into looking after somebody else.

Cruel though Richard's comments about her being a cardboard cut-out were, they had some truth – Susan tried to be a wonderful wife and mother *as she saw the roles*.

Penny

Penny, who looked after first her mother and then her invalid husband, eventually went to a self-help group for tranquilliser addicts. She very painfully came to realise that her parents had never been there for her; her mother because of her own drinking, and her father because he left the family. Feeling that it was her fault that her mother had so many problems, Penny sought to submerge all of her needs in the care of other people. Recovery from tranquilliser addiction was slow, but what was more painful was the eventual realisation that she had consistently denied having very real needs of her own.

Caroline

Caroline, who married Tim, the womaniser, was referred by her doctor to a sex therapist. During treatment, it came out that she had been sexually abused by her stepfather as a child, although she had no conscious memories of this. The great shame attached to the abuse had made Caroline deliberately seek out another abuser. Through therapy, she learned that she could not hope to change Tim's behaviour. All she could change was her own attitude. Her eventual decision was that there was no future in the marriage, and she and Tim were finally divorced.

Peter

Peter, the doctor, ended up in a hospital detoxification unit for alcoholism, as the 'little drinks' he took at the end of the day eventually got out of hand. Through treatment, he, too, came to realise that he suffered from codependency, resulting from his own family background of alcoholism.

Daniel

Daniel, who saw himself and his mother as such a very close unit, eventually ended up in a treatment centre for compulsive overeaters. This happened when he went for his annual medical check-up and was told by his doctor that his overweight constituted a serious health risk. He learned at the treatment centre that he had always tried to be a substitute husband for his mother – and that, in trying to meet her needs and making sure she would never go short of anything, had completely neglected his own.

STRATEGIES FOR COPING

Once it is pointed out, codependency can seem very obvious. So why does it continue to be so widespread? This is basically because of the denial which operates in all codependents. Once they are able to see the reality of their home backgrounds, can accept that these weren't as wonderful or perfect as they seemed, then they can begin to recover. Recovery is not possible in the face of high levels of denial.

Perhaps you are beginning to look at your history, your relationships differently. Maybe some of your denial is melting as you are coming to understand more about how codependency masquerades as normal behaviour.

In the early days, it was denial of the family problems which enabled the child to survive; as an adult, it continues to be used long after the need for it has evaporated. Codependency, like the order you put your socks on in the morning, or the way you brush your teeth, has become an ingrained pattern – and goes on being one. You don't 'grow out' of codependency. You have first to recognise and acknowledge that you have a problem and then seek help to break the habitual responses of a lifetime. It isn't easy; it *is* possible.

There are actually three aspects to what goes on in the mind of a codependent:

- The first is *minimisation*, where you say to yourself, 'it's not that bad'. You may have just lost your job, your husband may have just left you, but 'it's not that bad'. In the end you can minimize yourself into not 'existing' at all, but this is in extreme cases.
- The second is *denial*, where you tell yourself it's not even happening. An alcoholic will frequently blame other people for driving him to drink – but for that other person, the assertion goes, there would be no alcohol problem. Codependents deny that their family background was anything but perfect – they refuse to look at what it was really like.
- The third, most dangerous aspect is *delusion*, where everybody else is at fault except yourself. This is what

happens in the end in most codependent relationships. The reason they break down is because of *his* drinking, *his* womanising, *his* workaholism. If only, the codependent says, *he* would change, then I'd be all right.

Because codependents don't know how to get their basic needs met, they use other things, either chemicals, places or people to try and remedy the situation. But unless they can address the basic dilemma, their sense of self-esteem and self-worth will remain low.

Most codependents are full of fearfulness – terrified of other people and what they might do – so they employ any strategy they can to be in charge of other people's lives. We can see this clearly operating in the five case histories.

In Susan's childhood, her father had not been there. So, as an adult, she determined that her husband would always be there for her. What better way than to accompany him wherever he went?

Penny, unconsciously, felt that her mother was controlling her when she was a child. Because her mother was so frequently drunk, everything in the household revolved around her. Then in later life, Penny got control – although in a peculiar kind of way Mother was still in charge. But what better kind of husband than one confined to a wheelchair? You can surely control somebody like this – they can't even run away from you.

Under the guise of being a caring, concerned doctor, Peter controlled his patients. He chose to become a doctor partly because the profession gave guaranteed high status, and partly because it gave him control over other people. He had the sense that he had to control people, otherwise they would control him.

Of course, these thoughts, although very powerful, are only what is going on in the codependent's mind. It is not the case that Peter's patients want to control him. But codependents have blunted and warped perceptions coming from their own perspective as children of tragedy. The St Joseph's team believe that essentially, all codependents are children of tragedy.

The issue of codependency must be addressed as a serious

problem in our society because it is impossible for anybody to fulfil their true potential as human beings unless they can come from a position of security and love. All codependents come from a background of fear and mistrust – emotions they have absorbed into themselves. They have not learned viable intimacy skills, which is why they will almost always pick people who are somehow unavailable as partners. Peter's wife, for example, has M.E., which means she is often unavailable for him.

Most codependents will blame the person they have married or otherwise formed a relationship with for not being there, not realising or admitting that they have chosen this person for complicated reasons of their own. Codependents are people who learned that communication and relationships were dangerous to them. The main things they learned as children were:

- Don't talk.
- Don't feel.
- Don't trust.

It is common for codependents to sexualise their feelings. Instead of relating to other people, they try to seduce them when what they really want is to be held and loved. In extreme circumstances they may even try to rape them. Seduction and rape are, after all, means of controlling other people – or they appear to be – and give expression to powerful repressed feelings.

In its most excessive form, people take severe risks with themselves, either with their health or with their money. Compulsive gambling is a disease of great shame. So is bulimia, the gorge-purge disease; here, the shame has become so great that in the end it has to be symbolically thrown out.

All diseases related to addiction are extremely difficult to treat, because the roots lie so deep in childhood experiences. But the addiction which most attracts the codependents is the one of playing happy families. This, too, can be like a drug with a similar addictive element. Codependents do want to love and care for others – they just don't know how to do it appropriately. They have the right impulses, but they have been distorted along the way.

Fortunately, there is light at the end of the tunnel – recovery is possible. Some people may be helped by going to a suitable therapist or counsellor. *All* therapists specialising in codependency will have been through the mill themselves – and there are now also a number of self-help groups, mainly operating on the 12-step programme originally formulated for Alcoholics Anonymous – which can also enable people to recover from the syndrome.

But before moving on to recovery, it is helpful for any reader who wants to get to the bottom of codependency to have an understanding of the alcohol connection – something which is far more pervasive and devastating than is generally realised in a society in which most joyous occasions are celebrated with a drink.

3 ‖ The alcohol connection

As we explained at the outset, the term codependency was first used to describe people who formed relationships with alcoholics or heavy drinkers, and then wrapped their lives around these individuals and, more specifically, their problem. The reason that codependency was discovered through alcohol studies was that, in the end, most alcoholics are forced to seek treatment of one kind or another. Either they fall foul of the law because of their drinking, or their health suffers so badly that they have to be admitted to hospital.

Thus alcoholics provided excellent subjects for study; by the time their lives had become unmanageable, and their health had broken down through their incessant, uncontrolled drinking, they had become captive patients. As alcoholics began to be studied seriously in America, where more intoxicating liquor is probably drunk than anywhere else in the world, several factors emerged time and again:

● Alcoholism was almost always a disease of the family, rarely existing in isolation.
● Alcoholics tended to produce alcoholics.
● If such families did not produce active drinkers, they tended to breed codependents, the 'enablers', those who felt it was their mission in life to rescue or reform or control the drinkers in their lives.

58

- It is estimated that around 50 per cent of alcoholics come from alcoholic backgrounds.
- *Alcoholism is above all a disease of denial.* Although it might be obvious to onlookers that a particular person was an alcoholic, the drinker would persistently deny that this was the case. Even in codependent families where there was no obvious alcoholism, denial of painful realities and pretend happiness was something they all had in common.
- Alcoholism was a sickness of the spirit, a way of anaesthetising or dealing with emotional pain, felt long before actual alcoholism became a problem. This sickness could manifest itself in many kinds of addictive or dysfunctional behaviour. People brought up in such families, where the actual situation was forever denied, might suffer from eating disorders — compulsive overeating, anorexia or bulimia — excessive gambling, excessive womanizing or nymphomania, workaholism, grandiosity, defiance, rebelliousness, sexual abuse, paedophilia, shoplifting, religiosity — the symptoms and signs are many.

Anybody who has been made sad, ill or put under stress by the behaviour of somebody close to them has at least a tinge of the codependency syndrome — whether or not alcohol has played a part. Alcohol, although a terrible mind-altering drug, is still only one outward sign of something being badly wrong inside.

CHEMICAL DEPENDENCY

The thread that seems to run through all dysfunction and codependency is chemical dependency of one kind or another. And, as is becoming increasingly clear, people who do not drink or who are not addicted to drugs or overeating may manufacture their own internal chemicals by their behaviour.

People who often fall in love and then experience all the agony and ecstasy of this state may well be experiencing an adrenalin high. Raging codependency, where one's entire satisfaction seems to come from caring for others, can also bring about a high. Sex addiction can do the same. You don't have to be addicted to alcohol – it's just that alcohol provides extremely dramatic examples of how the disease sets in and gets gradually worse.

(Note: the authors are not concerned to try and turn everybody into teetotallers, or to condemn the demon drink. It is accepted that fine wines, a cold beer on a hot day, and drinking in moderation to enhance a meal or social occasion is a million miles removed from the kind of alcohol dependency which shatters family life and brings about the early death of alcoholics. To make the distinction clear, we define alcoholism as drinking for the sole reason of arriving at a state of oblivion.)

FAMOUS LITERARY ALCOHOLICS

It is comparatively easy to study alcoholics, partly because they present so often at hospitals or psychiatric wards, but also because many have been men (or women) of genius or towering talent, people whose lives and work have been studied in close, academic detail. Of seven American winners of the Nobel prize for literature, five – Sinclair Lewis, Eugene O'Neill, William Faulkner, John Steinbeck and Ernest Hemingway – were alcoholic.

Many other leading American writers also suffered from the disease. Famous literary alcoholics include: Dorothy Parker, Dashiell Hammet, Carson McCullers, Edward Arlington Robinson, Robert Lowell, Malcolm Lowry, Truman Capote and Jack London.

Addiction to alcohol is not confined to writers – the painters Mark Rothko, Jackson Pollock and Franz Klein were also alcoholics. But as the writers have left behind a huge body of writing, including much about drink, their work gives valuable insights into the insidiousness of the problem.

In an interesting study, *The Thirsty Muse*, American literature professor Tom Dardis examines the impact of alcohol on the lives of four great American writers – William Faulkner, F. Scott Fitzgerald, Eugene O'Neill and Ernest Hemingway. In all of these writers, their addiction to the bottle led to an early decline in their powers and only one, O'Neill, achieved greatness when past his forties. This was because he gave up drinking for 20 years, long enough to write his masterpieces examining the evils of addiction.

In spite of the massive talent and genius of these four men, they all denied their alcoholism. They blamed others, they minimised their drinking and its effect, they were horrible to their wives and friends. Alcohol turned them into monsters and the more monstrous they became, the greater became their denial.

Fitzgerald blamed his wife Zelda, also an alcoholic, for driving him to drink: 'The regular use of wine and aperitifs was something I dreaded but she encouraged because she found I was more cheerful then and allowed her to drink more.' Zelda spent many of her adult years confined to a sanatorium, after three severe breakdowns.

Eugene O'Neill, author of *Long Day's Journey into Night*, dealing with addiction, came from a family of alcoholics and co-alcoholics. His father, the actor James O'Neill was alcoholic, his mother became drug-dependent and his brother Jamie drank himself to death. O'Neill's son Shane also became an alcoholic.

In spite of his insights into alcohol and the devastation it can wreak, as is common, O'Neill blamed a woman for driving him to drink. 'There were many times, indeed, when she urged me to drink' he wrote to his attorney when his second wife, Agnes Boulton, pressed for more money in their divorce settlement. Like most drunken husbands, O'Neill would turn abusive and physically violent towards Agnes.

Agnes, a true codependent, as was O'Neill's later wife, Carlotta, came to feel that the rages, the alcoholism, the health problems and the difficult lives they led were part of the price for being married to a genius. O'Neill, like Fitzgerald, would not allow his wives to express their own creative talents. He wrote of Agnes:

She was always intensely jealous of my work as compared to what she could do. . . . I took (her) on when she was a cheap fiction writer, with no status of any kind.

Fitzgerald was furious with Zelda for taking 'his' subject (psychiatry) when she wanted to write a novel of her own. In the 1920s she wrote stories and articles which were published under Scott's name: the behaviour of a true codependent.

In America, there has always been a notion that alcohol somehow enables great creativity to come out, that it lubricates the psyche so that insights, otherwise inaccessible, will rise to the surface. This has been the thrust of most biographies of America's great writers and has helped foster the idea that there is something darkly glamorous about hard drinking – although time and again it ends in a tragic diminuition of talent – and an untimely death.

Tom Dardis dispels this notion once and for all in his book. The wonder, he says, is that these men were able to write at all, given the vast amounts of liquor they consumed, the days and weeks when they were often in detoxification centres or alcoholic comas, and their vast denial of the problem. In the end, he says, their alcoholism destroyed their ability and brought their talents to an untimely end.

It's not just major literary talents that have been destroyed by alcohol. A cliché of American movies is the whisky-sodden doctor who rallies round against all the odds to deliver the baby. This cliché has more than a grain of truth. Dr Joseph R. Cruse, the husband of Sharon Wegscheider-Cruse, and now one of America's leading experts on addiction and codependency, describes in *Painful Affairs* how his own alcoholism gradually developed, was denied, and led to delusion and disease. His story offers us further insight.

IN LOVE WITH DRINK

Alcoholism, writes Dr Cruse, can follow exactly the same course as a passionate love affair. Indeed, by the end, alcoholics can only be in love with their drink – they have lost the facility to interact with other humans.

In the book, he tells how he felt severe emotional pain as a child and then, at the age of 18, came the magical remedy: alcohol. 'I immediately fell head over heels in love with it. Relief and reward came with it! I found it!'

He writes:

Denial is a major obstacle to the treatment of the alco-

holic, especially the alcoholic physician. In my mind
there are three kinds of denial that allowed me to pro-
long my excessive drinking and get into trouble with it:
Denial by my colleagues, by society and by myself.

It is very rare, even nowadays when so much is known about
alcohol, that a doctor will diagnose alcoholism in a patient.
Even if his patient is known to be a heavy drinker, this is
usually seen as merely incidental to the health problems that
it has actually caused. But how much rarer, says Dr Cruse,
that a doctor will admit his own drinking problems, even
though heavy drinking is now known to be a feature of the
medical profession in every western country.
This is what he says about denial:

The primary symptom of alcoholism is one's own denial.
Occasionally I would have short periods of discomfort
about my drinking, but I would resolve them by changing some of my drinking patterns. My ability to quit
drinking for varying periods of time allowed me to deny
that I was in trouble with alcohol . . . Financial success
helped reinforce my denial. My material well-being
never suffered from my drinking . . . As with many professional people, it's easy to mask the signs of
decompensation. I could decide how many patients I'd
see each day, if any. I could cancel dates and no one
thought anything of it. Everyone accepts the line that
'Doctors' lives are not their own.'
    I never considered myself an alcoholic at all. As I
performed certain manipulations, such as hiding bottles
in the inner pocket of my sports coat or sneaking extra
cocktails when I was rubbing my thermometer on the
pillow or faking a cardiac arrest, I simply felt like a
naughty little boy.
    I couldn't let myself see it any other way. I wasn't able
to handle the reality of my situation . . .

But eventually, the drinking – so much of it carried out in
secret – led to a suicide attempt. Self-loathing eventually
catches up with the alcoholic. But, as for so many alcoholics,
once in recovery and permanently on the wagon, the equally

debilitating and horrific disease of codependency can take over. 'I was recovering nicely from my chemical dependency,' he says, 'but my burning embers of loneliness, yearning and dependency on others continued and flared to an open firestorm as the swallowing disease of codependency took over my life.' Neither he nor his family, wife and three children, had any idea they were suffering from codependency; they all had a vague idea that something was wrong, or missing – but that it would probably get better by itself now that Father's drinking had stopped.

One of the reasons that codependency so frequently establishes itself around an alcoholic, according to Cruse, is that people with drinking problems have to occupy centre stage – in sickness or in health, *they* are the important ones. This was the case with Hemingway, O'Neill and Fitzgerald: nobody could be as important in their lives as they were themselves. Their wives, families, were secondary, satellites orbiting around the sun, the genius. This is of course grandiosity, now well known as an aspect of both alcoholism and codependency.

People coming from alcoholic or other types of dysfunctional homes are, says Cruse, stunted in their emotional growth. They grow up still exhibiting the drives, raw emotions and needs of adolescents. Such children, if left to their own devices, remain separated from their true feelings, and this enables them to deny the reality of their situation. They 'marry into pathology', because when the times come for them to think about marriage, they look for somebody who appears normal to them. It is impossible, confirms Cruse, to learn healthy coping skills from dysfunctional parents. This is one reason why alcoholics often breed alcoholics or other chemical dependents.

NATURE AND NURTURE

In the introduction to his book Tom Dardis denies that alcohol is a way of plastering over emotional pain. His view is that there is a genetic predisposition towards alcoholism which is then subject to environmental forces. In other words, if the person predisposed towards alcoholism never takes a drink, then the disease will not manifest itself and the individual will be normal. It's the alcohol, he believes, which causes the personality problems associated with heavy incessant drinking, because it changes body cells, metabolism, liver function and, eventually, brain function. But take away the alcohol and, provided it's not too late, the person will become normal again.

Those involved in codependency treatment, as at St Joseph's, and addiction studies do not take this view. Research and observation has shown that, although there may well be a genetic or inherited predisposition to alcoholism, there is also a spiritual emptiness, a yawning gulf where the self should be, which allows the individual to attempt to 'drown sorrows' or to medicate the deep emotional pain that is felt.

It is the St Joseph's view that although there is very likely a genetic predisposition to alcohol addiction in about 70 per cent of cases, this predisposition does not have a causative effect. Very many people who are genetically predisposed towards alcoholism do *not* develop a drinking problem, and conversely, some people who do become alcoholic do so without having any demonstrable neurological differences from anybody else. This is known from studying brain cells of deceased alcoholics. The path between genetic inheritance and the development of alcoholism is not necessarily simple and straightforward.

If this is the case, then we have to try and decide what might be the trigger for alcoholism, and why a significant number of raging alcoholics do not appear to have a genetic predisposition. It seems to come down to codependency in the end. If untreated, the codependency will continue even if and when the chemically or drug-dependent family member stops using or abusing. Here is a story from David's casebook to illustrate how alcoholism can develop in later life – when someone has been drinking socially and without problems for many years. If you have a tendency to go over the recommended daily limit for your sex, this is a warning you would be very wise to heed. Certainly, it is one of those situations where it is *not* so easy to be wise after the event; that is, when you have become an alcoholic.

MARION'S STORY

Marion, 48, lives in a very smart area of London and is married to a successful City banker. She has four children, aged 18, 16, 14 and four. The three older children are at boarding school.

Marion came to see David for her drinking problem, which had started eight years previously – following the death of her father. She had been a social drinker for 20 years, but the problem had now got out of hand, and recently she had become aware that the drinking caused mood swings, depression and irritability. The mood changes were in fact withdrawal symptoms, and, like all alcoholics, she found she could modify these only by taking more alcohol.

In the morning, when she was sober, Marion would feel guilty and ashamed and make promises to herself and to her husband that she would not start drinking again. However, by lunchtime she would have taken her first drink, 'to steady herself', and would ask herself why she should stop drinking just to please her husband. 'Who the hell is he,' she would think, 'to make sacrifices for?' She started to believe that if only he was willing to make more sacrifices for her, then the drinking problem would stop. By the time she came to see David, her regular intake of alcohol averaged 80 units – the equivalent of 40 pints of beer a week – well in excess of the 14 units a week recommended safe level for women.

(It should perhaps be recorded here that most alcoholics who come to St Joseph's for treatment drink far more than this, with one or two full bottles of spirits a day being quite usual, but Marion had recognised that unless she stopped, her drinking would escalate even more.)

She had previously made several attempts to stop drinking but all were ultimately unsuccessful. She had managed to stop drinking while pregnant with her youngest child, thus avoiding the foetal alcohol syndrome which would have been a high risk if drinking at this level had continued throughout the pregnancy. But following the birth, drinking was resumed after only one or two dry days.

The more she tried to control her drinking, the worse it became. She had previously attended some meetings of Alcoholics Anonymous, but had not persevered, although she had accepted the First Step (see page 90 for all 12 steps), which says that 'we admitted we had become powerless over alcohol, that out lives had become unmanageable'.

It is only when defeat and powerlessness are admitted that recovery can take place. Psychotherapy or other forms of treatment are useless while drinking continues, and are a waste of time. David established that Marion was at a stage where she was ready for recovery, and to take the necessary steps to abstaining from alcohol.

Once Marion was able to stop drinking, they discussed her childhood, and it soon became clear that she was still suffering from the effects of very traumatic early years, and that all the rage from that childhood was there intact. At first, she told David that her childhood had been 'fairly happy' – but the facts belie this completely.

Her mother died when she was four, and her father, who took over the job of looking after her, developed a serious illness when she was five. Because of this, she was sent to a Catholic boarding school where she was extremely unhappy. The nuns, seeing the child's distress, offered her cakes to comfort her. This, a common method of comforting sad children, became the prototype for her later developing chemical dependency, as it attempted to blot out misery by the use of a mood-altering chemical: sugar and white flour are powerful mood-altering chemicals.

These cakes were Marion's introduction to the possibility of masking pain with a chemical. Her father recovered from his illness – he was a steady, if not a problem drinker, and it is very likely his illness was alcohol-related – and remarried. He retained, though, a strong attachment to his first wife through his daughter, and constantly remarked how much Marion reminded him of her. Marion soon came to feel she was being loved not for herself, but because she reminded her father so much of his dead wife, of whom Marion had only the briefest of memories.

Marion responded by being angelic, the 'perfect daughter', never saying or doing anything out of place, to try and be the little angel of her father's wishes. This continued until he died at 66 – and the problem drinking began.

Marion was devastated by her loss, even though she was grown up and had a family of her own. Part of the grieving process, though, was for herself – she felt she had lost a significant part of herself when her father died, the angelic, idealised being she had remained for him.

The alcohol served to mask Marion's codependency which, during her father's lifetime, had manifested itself as being who her father wanted her to be. In doing this, Marion had closed off an important part of her own personality. Because her father had never properly grieved for his dead wife and had so wanted to hold on to the image of her, he would not allow Marion to grow and develop as she should. She became frozen in her mother's image, an image that her father, in a way, needed her to fit.

Because her father had not loved her for herself, Marion assumed that there was something deeply unlikeable in her character, something nobody must ever know about. So, as the years when by, she developed a 'false self' which was 'Mummy's replacement'.

Her rage and anger had resurfaced when her fourth child was born when Marion was 44. The presence of a young child in the house triggered off all her deeply-buried early memories but because they were so painful, they had to be medicated with alcohol and kept down. Every time they threatened to rise up, Marion resorted to drink.

Her own 'inner child' had been neglected and because of this she had a deeply ambivalent relationship towards her youngest son, so much younger than his brother and sisters. Although she loved this little boy, she was also resentful of him, mainly because of what had happened to her in her own childhood. This had not surfaced when her other children were small because then her father was still alive, and she was continuing to play the part of Mummy's replacement.

Recovery

Marion's therapy consisted of three times weekly one-to-one psychoanalytic psychotherapy. She talked about whatever came into her mind and David listened, reflecting back and occasionally interpreting her words and feelings in the context of her life story. Bit by bit, as safety developed, Marion began not just to talk about her experiences but to relive them in all their intensity, and David began to be experienced by her as a significant figure, for example her father, or disowned parts of her psyche.

As the experiences were relived Marion was able to grieve for her losses and to recover contact with her lost 'inner child'. As she came to identify with the 'inner child', she experienced undiluted infantile dependence upon David. This was extremely frightening and painful but a necessary progression in the therapy. David in effect became a replacement for the alcohol. He was loved and hated, feared and despised. Most of all she hated herself for her dependence upon him because it reminded her of the abandonment she had experienced when her mother had died and when her father had sent her away, and how she herself had abandoned the 'child within' to comply with her father's demand that she become her mother's replacement.

In time the pain eased and the shame and humiliation experienced in the face of her neediness softened as she reclaimed her 'inner child'. Her neediness and hope became acceptable to her, and manageable. The experiencing and letting go of feelings left in its wake healing and hope, and the aching, yawning hole within her lost its power and the compulsivity lessened.

This does not mean that Marion can return to social drinking or any further contact with alcohol. She will always be an alcoholic and a return to drinking would signal an arrest in the growing confidence and hope she had for herself.

In recovery, Marion learned to separate her own 'child within' from her young son, and it is now possible for her to establish a boundary between her needs and his needs, and not take out on him something which belonged to her own past. Through recovery, Marion could offer him a different, and better, kind of parenting from the one she herself had received. She cannot put back the clock for her own childhood, but she can – as any adult can – prevent the problem from being continued to the next generation.

ALCOHOLISM AND CODEPENDENCY

Some people, like Marion, try to blot out their pain with intoxicating liquor; others may intoxicate themselves with people. Whatever the substance, whatever the dependency, according to Joseph Cruse, the underlying problem remains the same: low self-esteem, a poor sense of identity, a chasm where real, genuine feeling should be and a sense of desolation so acute, so all-pervading, that some kind of pathological dependency seems the only answer, the only way out. And it always starts from the same place: a dysfunctional family where realities are denied, and appearances attempted to be kept up at all costs.

In a typical alcoholic family, says Cruse, the drinker will become 'blaming and shaming' of the spouse, and the spouse, in her turn, blames and shames the drinker. Children from alcoholic families, he adds, are often in such denial that they do not see their home situation as chaotic or abnormal. They normalise the situation as far as they can, and when this is impossible, they start to blame themselves for their problems. They cannot blame their parents, as parents must be perfect and have the child's best interests always at heart.

All types of compulsive behaviour are desperate attempts to separate feelings and to keep them under control, to medicate them. Bill Wilson, one of the founders of Alcoholics Anonymous, recognised as long ago as 1958 that alcoholism gave rise to the twin disease of codependency (although in those days, it had no name). He wrote: 'when we are completely and emotionally dependent on someone else, we must control them.' Our need for control, Wilson understood, arose from the fear that the other person would leave us, abandon us. When our self-worth is intimately tied up in our relationship with another person, it eventually withers and dies, so that we are left without any self-worth at all.

And although low self-esteem and low self-worth can flourish without the lubrication of alcohol, the presence of a mind-altering substance makes the whole pathological process that much easier to study. Children from alcoholic families, says Cruse, become ever more adept in their ability to control, repress and deny. The trouble is that such self-deception and covering up shows on their faces at an early age, so that, like the alcoholic, they look ravaged and used-up when still young.

Also, children from alcoholic families are particularly at risk of developing codependency, because alcoholism is still seen as shameful – it's something parents don't do. Parents don't get out of control from drinking, they don't become abusive from drinking. Parents aren't like that. Codependents are, above all, those who have bought and invested heavily in the myth of the happy family.

The main dysfunction that alcoholics and codependents share is an almost unfathomable capacity for self-deception. Since Freud, self-deception has been identified as one of the major defence and survival mechanisms. We have already seen how the origins of codependency arise in childhood self-deception. But, like any habit, unchecked it just gets worse and worse. The reason it is not always spotted in codependents, in contrast to alcoholics, is that there are few obvious warning signs, such as passing out in the street or being admitted to hospital to have your stomach pumped out and so on.

The capacity of self-deception arises, believes Joseph Cruse, because the brain has to focus elsewhere when large amounts of painful stimuli come at a rate too fast to be absorbed. Very often, a child from an alcoholic home will blot out completely the experiences of these early years, as will somebody from a home where they were sexually molested. Warning signs for doctors and therapists are when an adult does not seem to have any memories below the age of about seven.

In time, this self-deception comes to mould our actual personalities.

CHANGING ATTITUDES

One of the reasons why codependency now flourishes as never before is because we have denied and denied and denied both the reality and the consequences of any form of addictive or chemically dependent behaviour. In fact, such behaviours are now built into the very fabric of our society, and are, if not always exactly rewarded, certainly minimised in their devastating effects.

Although alcoholism is now increasingly being seen as a serious family disease in America, in Britain and Europe it is still very much regarded as a minority problem, affecting only a small proportion of people – the ones who end up in the gutter, or whose lives have become so difficult that they have to go to Alcoholics Anonymous. One of our big problems is that we persist in seeing the ability to knock back alcoholic drinks as somehow worldly and sophisticated. It's very 'manly' to drink beers and lagers, according to the advertisements; it's very sexy and sophisticated to drink rums or gins; it's young and fun to drink vermouth. Yet the reality is that all these drinks are toxic – doing the body no good, damaging the brain and altering perceptions into denial, if we're not careful.

At one time, it was mainly men who were the drinkers and the women, refused such chemical dependency by society, who became the enabler-type codependent, the moppers-up, the controllers and controlled. Now, women are increasingly becoming active drinkers, as they have gained financial independence, high-paying careers and move in circles where not to drink is not to be 'one of the girls'.

Drinking is pervading ever more our society. In the average television soap or drama, within 10 minutes or less at least one character is drinking. Two British soaps – *Coronation Street* and *Eastenders* – centre round pubs as the hub of social life. True, characters in these early-evening soaps don't drink very much, but they are still seen to be drinking some alcohol just about every day. In *Dallas* all social life revolves around bars or drinks cabinets.

Most addicts, as is well known to therapists, are 'multi-abusers'. Thus, the great majority of alcoholics are chain smokers. F. Scott Fitzgerald smoked so many cigarettes a day that people said he 'ate' them. Writer and journalist Jeffrey Bernard, the subject of the hit London play *Jeffrey Bernard is Unwell*, has also made the cigarette his accessory, and has been described as not so much smoking cigarettes (untipped) as 'wearing' them. Jeffrey Bernard is also a gambler and writes amusingly about the inevitability of losing.

One of the problems about such cross-addiction is that the people who are so addicted are very often amusing, clever, warm-hearted people. They have a raffish glamour, and also, most of us warm to the lovable sinner rather than to the cold-hearted non-addict who appears to have no weaknesses or vices. The gamblers and the alcoholics among us often seem to be so much more human than the teetotallers and those who will never risk losing anything on the roulette wheel or the racing track.

Some alcoholics become workaholics as well – the great American writers referred to earlier all had an amazing capacity for work, considering how much of their time was spent drinking or recovering from drinking bouts. Some also abuse drugs or other substances. And even if they manage to stop drinking, they will often resort to some other compulsive behaviour unless the underlying codependency is treated.

Although eating disorders are intimately connected with dysfunction and codependency, and are, as much as drinking, a way of medicating feelings, relatively few alcoholics seem to suffer from them. Most don't really care about eating, and will just stuff a sandwich or burger into their mouths. It has been thought that women suffer more than men from eating disorders, partly because food is a 'substance' easily accessible to them. Now, new research is emerging to show that the syndrome may be just as common in men – but that it is more denied.

Very often there will be alcohol somewhere in the home background of anybody who manifests a compulsion to eat, spend or work beyond the realms of what is needed to satisfy physical hunger, live comfortably or earn a good living.

America has often been called the alcoholic republic of the world – and so it is easy to imagine that the codependency and addictive behaviour having its roots in drinking is purely an American problem. Certainly, just about all of the literature and scientific studies on codependency have originated from America. In Europe and other Western countries, we have not yet taken on board the dangers associated with alcohol, and persist in seeing it as a relatively harmless, socially acceptable conversational lubricant. Because we do not want to look at the reality of alcohol, we have hardly addressed the problem of codependency. In our ignorance, we continue to deny and to re-enact dysfunctional patterns all the time.

Luckily, recovery is possible, either through the help of a therapist, or by going to a self-help group. In our next chapter we will look at how people, perhaps you, can recover, and form healthy relationships with other people.

Part Two

BREAKING FREE

4 ‖ What you can do by yourself

What if you recognise that you have traces of codependency, but don't feel that the condition is bad enough to require treatment, either by going to a self-help group, or seeing a professional therapist? What can you do to help yourself?

As we explained earlier, we all have a little codependency in our makeup, in much the same way that we all have traces of negative characteristics such as anger, greed and self-pity. But as codependency is progressive, even minor manifestations need to be monitored and addressed, so they never become serious enough to blight our life.

THINK POSITIVE

It is *not* possible to overcome codependent inclinations by willpower alone. Because the condition has gone deep into the unconscious, it will resist all negative instructions, such as 'I will not have mother to stay if I don't want to,' or, 'I just won't allow him to make me so unhappy.' Try instead resolving something like: 'I will decide when I want mother to stay' or: 'I can learn to contain my own emotions. I can be happy.' In this context negatives always have to be turned into positives if they are to work – and it does require constant practice and vigilance to rescue oneself even from incipient codependency.

77

The first thing to realise when you're determined not to be a puppet on a string any longer is that NO can be a complete and very effective sentence. The second is that you do not need to apologise for not acceding to every request. Saying NO (ie using a negative) is here giving a positive indication of your wishes in whatever matter is at issue. For example, if you are asked to meet somebody from the airport, and you would rather not, or it is inconvenient, say so – politely but firmly. Say something neutral like: 'I shall be at work that day, so I won't be able to meet you.'

Learn to monitor when people are imposing on you, and when you would actually enjoy helping them out. Always ask yourself, before acceding to any request: is this something I really want to do – or am I doing it because I need to feel loved and wanted? At first, it may not always be possible to distinguish between the two. But gradually, you will learn to discriminate – and you will gain respect from others for being strong-minded and definite.

Look at why you do things. Many of us are so conditioned by traditions that even when the reason for a particular tradition is no longer valid, we tend to persist in doing things in a certain way. We need to start questioning what we do and why we behave as we do. We do so many things without thinking – they have become a part of our daily habits and routines – and we are completely thrown if something happens to change the status quo. Or we fear our partners will be badly affected.

Look at the patterns in your everyday life. Try to remember how they started. What would happen if you disturbed these patterns? Realise that it may be possible to change behaviour without your world falling apart.

For example, perhaps you always cook Sunday lunch because your partner took up golf on Sundays, at a time when he was under pressure at work and very tense and anxious. Then it was a helpful 'therapy' and you benefited too, because he was easier to live with and become more relaxed. Those problems are over now, though, so why should you still be left to cook the meal? Maybe you would like to do something else.

Look at what is being taken for granted. What would happen if you were not there one Sunday? Would it be a disaster? Or would it just point out to him that he is taking liberties and taking you for granted? Would you be able to stand and deal with any resulting anger and upset? Indeed, would there *be* any anger or upset?

Air your feelings. Staying at home, inwardly fuming about a situation and never saying anything will get you nowhere. If you change your behaviour, your partner may change his. You could, for instance, decide to have the main meal in the evening instead, when you can prepare it together or take it in turns. At lunchtimes, your partner can eat a snack at his golf club – and you can be free to meet your own needs for recreation.

It is also important to be able to distinguish between being assertive and being aggressive. Aggression happens when we are not in control of our own behaviour, and feel we are being put upon. This leads us to become angry with others who are making what we see as being unreasonable requests.

Those who feel they cannot be assertive, that they must either be acquiescent mice or angry aggressors, may benefit from attending assertiveness training classes, now held at most adult education centres.

(Note: people suffering from severe codependency would probably not benefit from assertiveness classes until the codependency itself has been properly addressed. See following chapters.)

PERSEVERANCE PAYS OFF

Learning new ways of relating, new types of more functional behaviour, does take time, and there will probably be a certain amount of backsliding, at least in the early days, but if you persist it will gradually pay off.

A common problem for codependents is that when they ask themselves: what do I want, the answer is: I don't know. If your needs have never been met, you may not know what these needs are.

If this is so for you, it may be more helpful to ask: would this decision make me more comfortable inside myself, or less comfortable? Do I feel any resentment, anger or hostility when I have said 'yes'? Did I really mean 'no' but was too afraid to say it?

Another question to ask yourself constantly is: who will benefit from this action? Many parents believe it is a sign of caring to stay awake all night worrying about their offspring, when they are out late, or when they are taking exams, for instance. But, who does the sleepless night benefit? Is the child better off because his or her parents are awake worrying? Are the parents made happier by sleeplessness?

No? Then don't stay awake with worry! The worries will still be there in the morning or perhaps the reason for the worry will have passed. Buy a relaxation tape and learn how to let go of worries and relax. Many people read before going to sleep because the reading relaxes them until tiredness takes over.

BE GOOD TO YOURSELF

Constantly bear in mind that you are worth taking trouble over: you are worth a good education, a good appearance, a good job, good food and a comfortable roof over your head. You deserve these things, and should make sure that they are yours. It is not selfish or uncaring to see that your own needs are met.

Ask yourself: what would I really like to do with my life? If the answer is not clear, ask yourself what you most enjoyed doing at the age of 10 or 11, before the demands of the educational and examination system called for sacrifice of 'less important' preoccupations. If it was playing the piano, for example, set aside a time to play every day. You may never become a world-famous concert pianist, but you will be expressing yourself in a way that you enjoy. And don't forget that other people, friends and family members, will respect you far more when you respect yourself. They might even enjoy hearing you play!

Take trouble, too, with your appearance, and dress to please yourself, not simply to make yourself attractive, sexy or seductive to others. Trying to be what other people want through dress is never a recipe for happiness. Fortunately, because clothes nowadays can be so comfortable, and yet smart at the same time, being well dressed is easier than it has ever been. Rules for correct dress have become so relaxed that we can all please ourselves more than ever before.

Resist trying to become what other people want you to be. Anybody in your life who tries to change you is really saying: as I can't control myself I will try and control you. By the same token, don't attempt to control other people's behaviour – it's not your place. There's an ancient joke about what a wedding day is supposed to mean to a bride: Aisle, Altar, Hymn. (I'll alter him.) If you don't like certain aspects of a person when you first get to know them, and are desperate to alter them, then you are storing up problems for later life. Think carefully about *why* you want to change them.

Men and women often believe that, thanks to their loving care, their partners or prospective partners will be enabled to give up smoking, gambling or whatever. Of course they won't. If you ever feel the person in your life needs rescuing, particularly from him or herself – beware. Codependency is rearing its head again.

For most of us, freedom from codependency means constant monitoring of our own behaviour. Simply håving an understanding of what codependency is, and how it can wrap its subversive tentacles around every aspect of our behaviour, will help us to avoid these dangers.

THE SPIRITUAL ASPECT

Codependency thrives on materialism, investing in externals such as people, roles, status, but these are empty and unfulfilling, which probably accounts for the growing trend in our society to reject materialism and embrace spirituality.

In this context, 'spirituality' relates to the ability to be in touch with our inner selves, and to understand that we are, as people, distinct from the roles and parts we play, and how we relate to other people. It is an important aspect of recovery, whether you are slightly codependent or in need of outside help. Spirituality forms an important part of 12-step recovery programmes (see Chapter 5).

The main problem for codependents, as we have seen, is that they have no real idea who they are. They identify completely with their roles and relationships, because this is the only thing that they have ever known.

But in order to recover, you have to become you – have the confidence to be truly yourself. This can be hard, because most codependents and addicts don't like themselves very much. If they liked themselves more, they would behave in different, less dysfunctional ways. Becoming spiritually aware means that you learn to like yourself, to realise that in your innermost being, you are peaceful, likeable, trustworthy, generous, good-hearted – and that all the negative aspects are things which have been overlaid on to your character because there has been such pain. Awareness of spirituality, of yourself as connected to the entire universe, helps to enable that long-held pain to be removed.

EXTERNAL VERSUS INTERNAL ASPECTS

Most codependents have difficulty in understanding just what is 'them' and what are the external aspects. Externals are anything you have overlaid, any label you may have been given, or have given yourself. Anything that can be taken away from you is external to you. Even reputation, fame, success, achievements, are externals, not the 'real' person inside. Codependents tend to place undue importance on their homes, their clothes, their circle of friends, their cars – falsely believing that all these things define them as they would like to be defined. You can always lose your reputation, your car, your spouse, your home, your job. Then where would you be, who would you be?

Learning to focus on internal aspects, rather than who one might be in the world, does not mean that one should neglect to earn enough money, to wear nice clothes, to gain a good education or to have a harmonious home. All these things are important, and should be attended to.

In fact, the more self-esteem there is, the more likelihood that a good home, a good job, good relationship, will come one's way. But always, with a healthy person, there will be a sense of having the ability to exist separately from whatever has been achieved, whatever money has been made. There will never be the feeling that one's whole identity rests on material achievements, or that there would be total devastation without them.

The biggest difference between a codependent and a non-codependent is that the former will live the whole of his or her life compulsively, like an addict, even if there is no actual substance abuse involved. The relationship addict will form relationships compulsively, seeking to establish a sense of identity through a merger with somebody else. The codependent seeks relationships addictively in order to try and fill up an empty feeling inside. If only I could find Mr or Miss Right, the codependent believes, then I'd be happy. The trouble is, because the sense of self-esteem and identity is so low, the codependent unconsciously feels that he/she must be unworthy of a truly decent person, so will settle for almost anybody who comes along. Then there is so often the thought: if he/she likes *me*, there must be something wrong with this person.

And of course there often is. Because while the dysfunction continues, the only type of people likely to be attracted are other dysfunctional individuals. Because of their own lack of personal identity, a codependent will only ever feel happy around addicts or other codependents. Negativity attracts negativity, and codependent relationships can never work out because the two people are compounding each other's problems, rather than imparting any kind of strength. So what happens is that another relationship is sought, as compulsively as the last.

Although codependents can enact other kinds of compulsive behaviour, such as workaholism or overachieving, relationship addiction is possibly the most pernicious, because it is so often pursued in the name of love. In fact, most codependents' love affairs, pursued with such passion and dedication, agony and ecstasy, are more usually adrenalin highs.

All compulsive behaviour is likely to increase the amount of adrenalin flowing around the body, and the codependent can so often confuse this with genuine love. It might be that you can recognise this tendency and seek out situations in which the adrenalin flows for you. Highs, however, by their very nature, are followed by terrible lows – but when there is a sense of inner peace, a spiritual awareness, there is a lessening of the need for either the highs or the lows – life can be lived on a much calmer level.

At first, for the codependent, this may seem dull and boring, just as 'nice', non-addicted people can seem boring and predictable for the relationship addict. Robin Norwood describes in her book *Women Who Love Too Much* how relationship addicts always, inevitably, go after dysfunctional partners – because they are so addicted to excitement, attachment and rescue instead of genuine love and regard, they cannot see the real person, only the addictive behaviour. For codependents, it is the addiction they are attracted to, rather than the person.

If you begin to follow a more spiritual path and begin to accept your inner self, this vicious cycle can stop – and automatically, there is attraction to a healthier type of person. Spirituality here means taking care of oneself first. In the Bible, Jesus says: love thy neighbour as thyself – not *more* than thyself.

There can be no recovery without self-respect, as this colours every single action. If you respect yourself, you will respect your body – and therefore will be less inclined to destroy it with cigarettes, mood-altering chemicals or junk food.

NEW AGE 'SOLUTIONS'

It has been noticed by many researchers and commentators that addicts and codependents are often extremely nice people – highly intelligent, amusing, energetic, talented. But those most at risk of developing dependency problems are often those most desperate to get back to the core of their being – they recognise that there is something more there, but simply do not know how to access it, or what it is.

We are now in a period of time often known as the New Age, which many people interpret as being a return to spiritual values. But for the codependent, there lurk enormous dangers in New Age matters. All over the Western world now, New Age artefacts – crystals, spiritual healing, Eastern-based meditation organisations, paganism, alternative medicine – are flourishing. Their appeal is that they are less materialistic, more concerned with the 'inner person' than standard twentieth-century values. But beware. There are at least as many ways of being caught and trapped in the New Age as with the Old one, as many ways to become addicted and codependent.

We believe that the values embraced by New Age practitioners are not necessarily any more spiritual than those of the old age – in fact, they may be even more pernicious, because they are masquerading under genuine spirituality, when they may be anything but. Anybody who, through the course of this book, has recognised codependency in themselves should be extremely wary of anything which seems to offer an easy solution. There is no magic way to take away the codependent patterns of a lifetime.

Also be extremely wary of paying out huge sums of money, joining 'instant enlightenment' weekend courses, or putting your faith in a guru. However holy a guru or 'realised being' might appear, the fact is that they are just as human and fallible as you are, often more so. Genuine spiritual practitioners understand that there are huge dangers in 'Hollywood yoga' or in handing yourself over to the care of somebody who seems charismatic or to have a special understanding of the meaning of life.

Anybody with a codependent streak is in great danger of being taken in by a charismatic spiritual leader. They are all fallible – even though some may have developed genuine spiritual qualities. A true guru is somebody who can lead you from darkness into light – that is what the word means. It is important not to follow a 'rugu' – somebody who leads you from light into darkness, or a 'gugu' – somebody who keeps you in the dark. Any human being who insists that he (or she) is worshipped, and entitled to all your worldly goods, is not a truly spiritual person – just another codependent, desperate for your love and esteem.

Recovery, which is another term for embracing genuine spiritual values, will mean that there is no longer the same reliance on drugs, substances or people to provide 'highs' in one's life. Recovery means that you can appreciate the wisdom or spirituality of somebody else, that you can learn from them if they have something of value to teach, but that you will not ever come to depend or rely on them in the sense that you will never be tempted to hand over everything to them, in the belief that they will be able to take all your cares and woes away and enable you to have a worry-free, stress-free life. No human being can ever do that for another – all that a helper of any sort can do at best is to help you to see where the essence of your own identity lies, and to impart some useful strategies for accessing this and becoming aware of it.

Nobody, not even a therapist, religious leader, husband or wife, can give you the strength you lack yourself. Recovery is possible only when you can find your own source of strength, and act accordingly.

True spirituality means taking time for the things that matter to you, and not having your day filled out with catering for other people. This does not mean you have to be selfish – in fact, truly spiritual people are the most loving and giving. But they do not give in order to make you feel grateful, obligated or under a burden. They give because they have something to spare – but they rarely give at the expense of themselves. They give because they love you, and they love you because they love themselves.

When we reach adulthood we have to acknowledge that we, not others, are responsible for our own behaviour and the mistakes we make. Making mistakes is part of the human condition. We also have to be able to forgive ourselves and not lay blame either on ourselves or on others. The reason we made mistakes in the past was because we didn't know any better – an awareness of true spirituality helps us to know better and to be generous both with ourselves and with others.

This does not mean, of course, that we now tolerate bad behaviour on the part of others and excuse everything. But we can be tolerant to the person without condoning their behaviour. If they knew any better, they would not behave as they did. But we must also be careful not to cultivate a feeling of superiority, that we are better than other people. That is another sign of codependency, and arises mainly out of fear.

People who embrace a genuinely spiritual path find that it

is hard work. As anybody who embarks on a course of exercise finds that their muscles lose 'tone' if not kept fit, so the spirit loses 'tone' when spirituality is not practised. There has to be constant vigilance, otherwise old bad habits will be in danger of reasserting themselves. After all, we have held onto them for long enough – they are not going to relinquish their grip without a fight.

5 || Self-help groups

However serious or ingrained the codependency, however long there has been a problem, it is never too late to seek help. All professional therapists specialising in this field have themselves been either alcoholics, children of alcoholics or have suffered from codependency severe enough to make their lives at the very least extremely uncomfortable. They know what the problems are – they have been there themselves.

There are at the moment three main ways of beginning recovery:

- Joining a self-help group.
- Getting professional help.
- A combination of both.

If the problem has become very bad, so that addictions dominate your life or that of somebody you love, it may be appropriate to seek professional therapy from somebody who understands the process. It should be said here that by no means all psychiatrists, doctors and therapists accept the view of addiction and codependency outlined in this book. The concepts are still so new that many counsellors and therapists have never come across or studied the body of research now available. The St Joseph's Centre for Addiction, fully described in the following chapter, offers a comprehensive range of help.

Of course, in order to get to a therapist or self-help group, you have to know, or suspect, that you have a problem which needs expert help. If there is obvious alcoholism or drug addiction this might be easy – but where there is no such substance abuse, it becomes more difficult.

So before going any further, answer this simple quiz which will give an indication as to whether or not codependency might be a problem for you. Just answer yes or no to the following questions:

- Do you often feel frightened and nervous of other people?
- If you see a fight in the street, does your heart beat faster as if you are somehow responsible for it?
- Do you constantly want approval from other people?
- Do angry people frighten you?
- Do you get very upset by personal criticism?
- Do you feel responsible for the other people in your life?
- Do you ever feel your family would fall apart without you?
- Do you ever feel guilty when you stand up for yourself instead of giving in to the wishes of others?
- Do you find it hard to refuse a request for help?
- Do you tend to attract people who seem to need a lot of help?
- Would you call yourself a perfectionist?
- Do you tend to be your own sternest critic?
- Do you seem to come alive in a crisis?
- Do other people see you as one who copes wonderfully?
- Do you ever feel that other people don't appreciate all you do for them?
- Do you ever feel that people tend to abandon you through no fault of your own?
- Would you call yourself a very loyal person?
- Do you find it difficult to have fun?
- Do you always try to avoid conflict instead of facing up to it?
- Do you ever feel you could have been more successful if other people hadn't got in your way?

The more yes answers, the more codependent you probably are. But codependency is not a life sentence. You can free yourself from the chains that bind you to other people – without dismissing them from your life.

SELF-HELP GROUPS

Sometimes, a problem may be so severe that professional therapy is needed before self-help can be started. For others, self-help programmes work wonderfully on their own. The main reason that self-help groups can work so well is because everybody in the group has been in the same boat, whatever their background, social class, educational level or attainments. And although people may deny the problems to themselves, or to their doctors and their families, they can't deny them to the group – all members know every trick and denial there is, so it's impossible to pull the wool over their eyes.

THE 12-STEP PROGRAMME

All self-help groups which address codependency – or indeed any other form of dependency – are based on the famous 12-step programme, originally formulated for Alcoholics Anonymous more than 50 years ago. Here, for the benefit of those people who are not familiar with them, are the 12 steps for recovery from addiction:

1 We admitted we were powerless over alcohol (eating, people, gambling, narcotics) and that our lives had become unmanageable.

2 We came to believe that a Power greater than ourselves could restore us to sanity.

3 We made a decision to turn our will and our lives over to the care of God *as we understood him.*

4 We made a searching and fearless moral inventory of ourselves.

5 We admitted to God, to ourselves and to another human being the exact nature of our wrongs.

6 We were entirely ready to have God remove all these defects of character.

7 We humbly asked him to remove our shortcomings.

8 We made a list of all the people we had harmed and became willing to make amends to them all.

9 We made direct amends to such people wherever possible except when to do so would injure them or others.

10 We continued to take personal inventory and when we were wrong, promptly admitted it.

11 We sought through prayer and meditation to improve our conscious contact with God *as we understood him*, praying only for knowledge of his will for us and the power to carry that out.

12 Having had a spiritual awakening as the result of these steps, we tried to carry this message to others, and to practise these principles in all our affairs.

At first, some of these 12 steps may sound distinctly odd, irrelevant or out of date. They may also appear offputtingly religious and sanctimonious. But the important thing is that, whatever they may sound like at first – they work. They've worked for 50 years. So what do they involve, and how should we interpret them?

Alcoholics Anonymous – the 'anonymous' group that started it all and provided a prototype for all subsequent 12-step fellowships – first came into being when two alcoholics in America got together to see if they could find any way of recovering from the illness (in that they regarded their alcoholism as an illness) that was ruining their lives, and was, indeed, threatening to kill them prematurely. The two men had already been to drying-out centres, and treated for their addiction many times. But they had always returned to the bottle.

The first important discovery these two alcoholics made was that they needed each other. What they could not accomplish on their own, or even with the help of doctors or psychiatrists, they found they could achieve together, just because they had the same problem and gave each other support and encouragement. They also discovered that recovery actually became possible in the company of other alcoholics – a revolutionary idea which is still considered controversial.

Some professionals working in the addictions field are enormously resistent to 12-step groups, believing that it is not possible to become well merely by associating with other addicts. There also remains considerable doubt over how much patients can help themselves recover without professional intervention. Alcoholics Anonymous and the other, newer 12-step programmes have turned on its head the idea that 'experts' are always needed, and have produced a body of expertise and knowledge based simply on the struggles of fellow sufferers. If necessary, professionals may be called in to play a secondary, supportive role – instead of being called in first.

It is because 12-step programmes have been so successful in helping people to recover from addictions – often without any intervention from doctors or other therapists – that we have put the self-help section first.

The true experts on addiction and codependency are those who have suffered themselves – nobody else can truly know the extent of the denial, the cover-up, the collusion, the enabling, the retreat from reality, the excuses and promises that are made, the chaos that can descend when a person is in the grip of an addiction.

There still persists a lingering belief among those not chemically dependent that addicts could 'snap out of it' and 'pull themselves together', if they exerted more will-power. The *first step* in the self-help programme admits this to be impossible. We were powerless, it says – we admitted our lives had become unmanageable.

One of the most important aspects of the original, first Alcoholics Anonymous group – still strictly adhered to today – was the 'anonymous' element. Within the original group, nobody was identified except by first name. Nothing else was known about any member of the group. The only knowledge needed was that each member was ready to admit their powerlessness over alcohol. The other essential feature was that the groups were not led by any kind of 'expert' – the experts were the drinkers themselves. They knew far more about their problem than any doctor or other therapist – once they had the courage to admit that they had a serious problem.

STEP-BY-STEP 'RECOVERY'

The two founders of AA realised that in order to recover from alcohol, or indeed any addiction, the addict had to be able to admit being defeated by the substance. Many addicts like to imagine that they are in power over their addiction and can give it up any time they like – it's just that they choose not to. The founders of AA realised this was nonsense, but that once powerlessness over the substance was acknowledged, this enabled a remarkable transformation to take place in the attitude of those chemically dependent. Instead of lapsing into self-pity the individual became ready to look at the effect of the drinking or other chemical using on his or her life, and could start to think about recovery.

From the first, the AA concept of alcoholism was of an illness, a disease of mind, body and spirit. Now, for all 12-step programmes, including those for codependency, there is the same concept of an illness.

After Step One, Steps Two and Three become important. *We came to believe that a Power greater than ourselves could restore us to sanity*, and *We made a decision to turn our will and our lives over to the care of God as we understood him.*

Some people take exception to these aspects of the 12 steps, seeing them as too overtly Christian and patriarchal, or as constituting some kind of fundamentalist or born-again religious sect. In fact, they have nothing to do with organised religion, and one does not have to believe in any kind of otherworldly God to accept them.

The steps are very logically arranged. If, in Step One, we acknowledge that we have become powerless over the substance, and that because of this our lives are unmanageable, it follows that we must reach out to somebody or something greater than ourselves if we are to be helped to recover.

Step Two allows us to acknowledge that help is at hand and that we are not alone in our struggle. Some people attending 12-step fellowships see this 'higher power' as the group itself, the struggles of all the others. Many sufferers have found that the 'power of the group' is far, far greater than any they could access by themselves. It is not necessary to believe in any formal religion to acknowledge the existence of a 'higher power'. We all know that groups can be far more powerful than individuals at achieving whatever aims are held to be in common. By themselves, workers often have no power, and can be ruthlessly exploited by employers. But if workers form unions or groups, they can become powerful against the employer, and formulate rights and conditions to which employers may have little choice but to accede. In addiction, the 'ruthless, exploitative employer' is the dependency on a substance or relationship.

One of the earliest slogans of the present-day feminist movement was 'sisterhood is powerful'. Here again was the same idea at work. When denied education and economic independence, women by themselves were powerless, but when they got together, and united with common aims, they quickly learned that much can be achieved.

The group idea is also behind the much longer established old boys' networks, all associations and pressure groups. The revolutionary concept of AA was that it harnessed the group idea to aid recovery from an illness.

In order to accept Steps One, Two and Three, there has to be humility, something which is brought out in Step Seven. While there is arrogance and ego, there can be no recovery. There has to be a willingness to recover, and while in hot denial of their problem, many addicts will continue to assert that they have chosen this way of life, that they like it.

But what about Step Three, which actually mentions the existence of God? Very many people have stumbled over Step Three – imagining that this means they have to dedicate their life to some religious pursuit, perhaps substituting one addiction for another.

But that is to misunderstand this very important step. It is basically the acknowledgement that there has to be some kind of ongoing relationship between oneself and the higher power, or God *as we understand him*. Coming to terms with this Step involves sorting out who, or what, your particular higher power could be.

One addict who had enormous difficulties with Steps Two

and Three had a Catholic mother and a Protestant father. He was brought up in a working-class area of Glasgow, and came to believe that religion divided people rather than bringing them together. He could not see how he could make use of a spiritual programme; even the mention of God made him feel full of rage.

How could he come to terms with Steps Two and Three? At meetings, he remembered that because of his drinking, his wife had thrown him out of the house and, for a time, he had lived in a shed at the bottom of his garden. When he came home from the pub, he would stumble into the shed and fall into an alcoholic sleep. Because he had no human to talk to at these times, he started talking to the lawnmower in the shed. It was during one of these heart-to-hearts with the lawnmower that he finally made up his mind to seek recovery.

He had come to the point where he knew that unless he did attempt recovery, he would lose everything. That was his lowest point – all addicts have to reach their personal 'lowest point' before they can start to recover – and the very next morning, he sought help. He came to realise that, in a peculiar way, the lawnmower had been his 'higher power', the means by which he was enabled to look outside himself for help. For this addict, the lawnmower experience became 'God as he understood him', and from then on, he could forget about the religious implications and work through the steps.

In fact, the 12-step programmes constitute the only self-help system (that works) whereby those of any religion or none can join together in a spiritual union. The whole basis of the fellowships is that they are respectful and tolerant of each member, whatever their background or religious beliefs. What unites the group is its powerlessness over the addiction.

To summarise so far, Step One says: I can't; Step Two says: I am not alone; and Step Three says: I can be helped.

Steps Four and Five call for honesty and openness, and action to shed our secrets.

In Steps Six and Seven, we take full responsibility for our problems and shortcomings (NOT the same as taking blame) and get help from our 'higher power', in order to change ourselves.

Steps Eight and Nine ask for amends to be made to those we have injured or hurt – often a very hard and painful thing to do. As we have seen in Chapter 3, addicts of all kinds blame others for their problem.

Step 10 acknowledges the 'one day at a time' aspect of all these self-help programmes, admitting that continuous vigilance is required, otherwise there may be a danger of slipping back into old, addictive habits.

Steps 11 and 12 acknowledge that continous contact with the 'higher power' must be maintained, and that, once recovery has been set in motion, it is important to reach out and share the insights that have been made possible by following the steps.

The whole point about a self-help 12-step programme is that recovery proceeds by means of similarly afflicted people working together in groups. The various 'Anonymous' organisations do not raise funds, they do not promote themselves, and they do not identify names of group members. There are now very many of these groups, ranging from AA to Al-Anon and Ala-Teen (for family members of alcoholics) to Families Anonymous for families of drug addicts, Narcotics Anonymous for those using illicit drugs, Adult Children of Alcoholics, for grown-up children of alcoholics, Overeaters Anonymous and Codependents Anonymous – and all work in much the same way.

CODEPENDENCY GROUPS

In Anonymous groups for codependents, the principal defences of denial and minimisation are gradually broken down. By attending the fellowship regularly, isolation is also broken and secrets no longer have to be kept. This means that shame and fear can be lessened, by bringing them out into the open. The rigid 'Don't Talk' rule system which has in the past supported the dysfunction fades away as people start talking about their problems – something few have done before.

Members of 12-step fellowships are encouraged to express their feelings – whatever these might be. Nobody is judgmental or condemnatory in a group, and so they begin to defeat the major 'Don't Feel' rule which governs the lives of most codependents with an iron rod.

Thirdly, the 'Don't Trust' rule is broken as sufferers learn to trust the others in their group, safe in the knowledge that whatever they say will not be repeated outside and will not be held against them. Many codependents, and other addicts, have felt they have 'come home' when joining a 12-step programme, even if they felt beforehand that there would be nothing in it for them.

One woman, a compulsive gambler who reluctantly joined Gamblers Anonymous when her money, house and belongings had all gone, said: 'I didn't want to go at first, because I felt I would have nothing in common with the other gamblers there. But when I went, I realised that I had everything I needed in common – we shared the addiction, and that was enough.'

Another important aspect of 12-step programmes is that they provide a new family, a family of choice. However horrendous our own home background has been, there is little we can do to change it. We cannot have different parents, or have come from a different environment, and there is not much point in wishing that we did, or that we could put the clock back. But the fellowship provides a new family which, instead of sabotaging, being negative or unsupportive, can become the kind of sustaining, nurturing family which the child within the adult can use to foster growth. It is never too late to find a new family or to live anew your childhood, as so many sufferers from addiction or codependency have discovered.

Codependents, particularly, can learn the all-important 'three Cs' in relation to their own form of addiction. They come to understand that:

- They did not *cause* other people's behaviour.
- They cannot *control* others.
- They cannot *cure* them.

The hardest lesson for codependents to learn is that they are powerless over other people's behaviour – although not over their own. Through the support of the fellowship, they can learn to 'detach with love' so that those closest to them become free to make their own choices in life, their own mistakes, and take their own path. We may not like or approve of the choices those near to us make, but there may be little we can do to influence these. Other people are not extensions of ourselves, but individuals in their own right.

It is important that if you have recognised yourself as codependent, but are also chemically dependent, you should tackle the substance addiction first. If you have, or feel you have, a drinking, eating or drugs problem, it is advisable to go to the appropriate Anonymous group first, as it is actually impossible to use a Codependents Anonymous recovery group until all chemicals have been put down. (An exception is usually made for smoking cigarettes; although not condoned, nicotine is not seen as a mood or mind-altering drug in the same way as alcohol or psychotropic drugs.) Very many people find, in recovery, that they are suffering from codependency in addition to their active addiction.

JOINING A GROUP

Those not dependent on a mood- or mind-altering substance or activity, can proceed straight to a suitable Anonymous fellowship. It is important to try more than one group, if you possibly can as, although there are always common aims, and all groups work the 12-step programmes, there are differences from group to group.

The Anonymous groups which are suitable for codependents are: Codependents Anonymous and Adult Children of Alcoholics. It is almost certain that anybody coming from an alcoholic background will grow up codependent. Research now suggests that those who seem to escape codependency while coming from the kind of background which encourages this condition, are people lucky enough to have someone or somewhere else to escape to. In other words, they are not continually at the mercy of their using or otherwise dysfunctional parents, but have a granny, an aunt, a nanny or other family member who can be supportive and take off some of the strain.

Groups vary in size and composition. Some are large and

relatively impersonal, others are small and more intimate. Some people feel more comfortable meeting in small groups of just five to seven people, and prefer to gather in the living room of a member's house rather than the anonymity of a church hall. Others prefer larger groups in public halls or clubs. There are special groups for women only, and also groups for beginners to the 12-step programmes. Anybody who is interested should ask to attend an open meeting first. Most meetings are for members only – and others are specifically designed for people who may just wish to try them out. (See pages 137–139 for suitable contact numbers.)

No 12-step programme is a 'quick fix' or a magical solution to all life's problems. When people first go along to meetings, they may feel ambivalent and confused, rather than happy and at peace instantly. Unlike some spiritual groups, 12-step programmes do not claim to offer instant enlightenment.

Sufferers should be prepared for various aspects of recovery to be painful. If pain was not involved, we would not have needed to deny, minimize or medicate our problems in the first place – and there may be a relapse or regression. Breaking the pattern of a lifetime will take time and understanding. Any action, repeated often enough, gets into the unconscious so that eventually we do not know we are doing it, and it becomes removed from conscious choice. Think how many people have nervous habits and tics which they don't consciously know about – the habit has become so much a part of them over the years.

Recovery may also mean taking a hard look at existing relationships, and asking whether they can continue in their present form. Don't forget, also, that the people around a codependent often have a great vested interest in the behaviour continuing (see Introduction), and they may actively sabotage attempts at recovery.

In Anonymous fellowships, recovery is often made easier by forming a non-dependent relationship with a 'sponsor' – somebody who has travelled further down the road of recovery than you have, but who understands every aspect of the disease from having reached rock bottom themselves. A sponsor is somebody who has successfully worked the 12-

step programme themselves, and can guide and encourage the newcomer. But again, there should be no reliance on the sponsor to bring about recovery – that is always a personal quest.

HARD WORK REWARDED

We do not underestimate the hard work involved in recovery but there is no doubt that it is worth it. Ask anybody who has recovered from codependency or any other addiction, and they will tell you without exception that life is better on the other side. For the first time in their lives, they are able to make choices, rather than being blown this way and that by their addiction or dependency. Also, there is a far higher sense of self-worth and self-esteem.

In recovery, people learn to love themselves. This enables them to make better relationships with other people, attract a better type of person to themselves, and to feel, possibly for the first time, a true sense of freedom, instead of being weighed down with nameless fears and anxieties and the endless quest to control.

General health will also improve. The enormous stress which characterises codependency can disappear, and this means more energy, a greater resistance to infection, and a greatly decreased risk of developing any stress-related disease, from heart disease and cancer to depression, anxiety and insomnia.

In recovery, people become able to set their own goals, based on their particular talents and abilities. They are able to take risks rather than play safe all the time. By this, we don't mean the excessive and stupid risks taken in gambling, but they become able to risk rejection, criticism and failure. They can do this because their sense of self-worth has become strong enough for them not to be devastated when things go wrong.

Life will still have ups and downs for the recovering codependent – but the vicissitudes can be handled in a healthy way. Other people will not be blamed. The sense of being worthless, of not having, or deserving, any needs, will greatly diminish. Recovering codependents are much nicer people because they no longer carry around a burden of hate and resentment of other people, the feeling that other people are responsible for their failures or lack of success in life.

Recovering codependents (we cannot use the word 'recovered' because in a sense, no addict or chemically dependent person can ever have finally recovered) can face the world from a position of strength, rather than one of weakness and fear.

The best aspect of recovery is that the rot can stop. Adults can stop passing codependent or addictive behaviour on to their children, who, in their turn, will grow up healthy enough to be good parents.

So there is nothing to lose, and everything to gain, from recovery from an age-old, inappropriate pattern.

BRIDGE TO THE OUTSIDE WORLD

One criticism that has been levelled at 12-step programmes is that they substitute one addiction for another: instead of being alcoholic, codependent, or whatever, critics claim, you become addicted to going to AA or CODA meetings. There is a certain amount of truth in this. If all your life you have lived addictively, this pattern is not going to be broken all at once. Many people whose lives have been governed by their codependency do go through a phase of complete identification with the 12-step programme, and can become so bound up in the wonder and delight of working the steps that they cannot see beyond the group.

Codependency goes so deep and can be so difficult to extricate, it may take many months – in some cases years – before the fellowship can serve as a proper bridge to the outside world rather than a refuge from the difficulties of ordinary, everyday life.

So how long should you expect to need a 12-step programme? There are no hard and fast rules, but usually the sufferer will know when a point of recovery has been reached so that the fellowship of the group is no longer needed. It is helpful to see the group as a substitute parent – there when needed but not to be relied on at all times. The eventual aim should be for freedom from the group, freedom to walk alone

– with the knowledge that, if needed, the group will always be there.

You may find that as you recover you need the group less and less, going perhaps a few times a year, or maybe just once a year. People who go to 12-step groups for years on end without appearing to recover, or being able to stand on their own, may well be in need of a different kind of help. Not everybody recovers by attending groups, although they have a remarkable record of success – far greater than that of any other addiction recovery programme.

Meetings tend to have a high emotional intensity. This is fine for those who feel they have reached a point where healing is needed, and where change will be welcomed. For other codependents, the high level of honesty and openness over emotions can at first be overwhelming, but do not be put off.

Remember that codependents have essentially lived their entire lives in an emotional desert and their previous relationships will have been based on pretence and insecurity. As a result these relationships, although they may seem intense and passionate at first, will be shallow and superficial. Because the codependent has many strategies for not allowing him or herself to be known, there can be no true intimacy in relationships. Because of this, to be suddenly flooded with feelings and emotions can be acutely painful and distressing.

Early in their recovery, most codependents go through a stage of blaming their parents for their present problems. This is only to be expected. It would be strange if, having broken through the pretence at last, you are not angry at the amount of time and energy which has been wasted in maintaining the 'happy family' charade.

It should be understood, though, that the viciousness with which the parents are despised, once the scales fall from their adult children's eyes, is actually a wish to turn the tables on them and become the aggressor instead of the exploited one, seek revenge for what they did to you when you had no way of escaping.

Parents become judged against an ideal of what they might have been. Most codependents in early recovery go down this road, and anger is often the very first hint that the wall of defence is cracking at last. But when there is more maturity in recovery, codependents see that this type of blaming is destructive and counter-productive, and will only hinder healing. They will understand that there is an inherent contradiction in trying to perpetrate the same behaviour towards their parents that was meted out to them. It doesn't matter who started the problem; the important thing is that the rot stops here.

True healing can begin when sufferers come to understand that, whatever the hideousness of the past, there is help and a close, supportive family available now. When the long-held 'victim' role is shed, there is no blaming, and parents can be forgiven. This does not mean that their behaviour is condoned. Often they behaved as they did because they knew no other way, or because they could not help it – not because they meant to harm.

It is very important in recovery that parents can be forgiven. But even this has to be correctly timed. If there is an attempt at forgiveness too soon, then this may be an attempt to avoid feeling pain and anger. If there are too-early attempts made to sweep all hurt away with 'peace and love', the underlying codependency may remain. Don't imagine that everything ends with death, either – many people carry around vengeful feelings towards their parents years after they died.

One codependent put her recovery like this:

> I came to understand that I had a normal response to an abnormal situation. I learned that my father's cruelty to me came not because I deserved it, or because he was a horribly mean person. It was the impotent striking out of a man who was very often under the influence of alcohol, hung over, or desperately trying to keep his alcoholism under control. This explanation eventually allowed me to admit what had happened to me without giving up my love for him, or his for me.

When codependency has been caused by alcoholism of one or both parents, it is important to understand that it is the pervasiveness of alcohol which has caused the problems, not the bad behaviour of the child or the wickedness of the parent. If it can be understood that the parent was in the grip of something which could not be easily controlled, early experiences can be reframed in a less harsh light. The addiction has got in the way of proper family relationships, and the addiction itself may have started because there were chronic relationship difficulties in the first place. At first, alcohol (or any other drug) can seem a useful way out.

Fellowships for Adult Children of Alcoholics or Codependents have also been criticised because it has been claimed that they lay emphasis on the least healthy aspect of a person, accentuating the negative rather than the positive. It has been argued that the label Adult Child of an Alcoholic encourages people to define themselves by the most destructive thing that ever happened to them. Others have argued that self-help groups demand too much conformity to the group's aims. There is a grain of truth in both these criticisms, but it should be realised that 12-step groups are themselves only a step on the way to recovery. The important thing that they do is to help sufferers understand the reality of their plight.

Until this can be acknowledged, there will be no recovery – it won't magically happen unless drastic and important steps are taken. Codependency won't suddenly disappear of its own accord – it has to be helped away by a programme of action and attitudes specifically designed to combat the problem.

Let's now take a closer look at one of the principal avenues available for codependents, the fellowship of Adult Children of Alcoholics, before examining the role of professional help in the recovery process.

ADULT CHILDREN OF ALCOHOLICS

This self-help programme, based on the 12 steps, acknowledges that children of alcoholics themselves often have particular problems which may not be addressed by attending ordinary meetings. Indeed, the first ACOA meetings in the UK were set up by Al-Anon members who recognised the special needs of children of alcoholics. Since their early days some groups have constituted themselves separately from Al-Anon and called themselves ACA. For the newcomer the differences between ACOA and ACA are trivial and will not affect the path of early recovery.

ACOA proceeds from the belief that children from alcoholic parents are not allowed to be real children – that is, valuable, worthy of esteem, imperfect, dependent, immature. Instead, they are expected to become little adults and are shamed by the parents when they cannot behave like adults. As a result, they never really grow up, but are emotionally stuck in childish ways of behaviour.

Alcoholic families have rigid rules which, as we have seen, can be expressed as: Don't talk, don't feel, don't trust. This leads to particular characteristics in the children. These include:

- Being afraid of authority figures.
- Becoming approval-seekers and people-pleasers.
- Being frightened by angry people and by criticism.
- Finding addictive or compulsive people to marry or form partnerships with, time and again.
- Feeling that they are a victim.
- Finding it easier to be concerned with others than looking after themselves.
- Getting guilt feelings when standing up for themselves.
- Being addicted to excitement and drama.
- Judging themselves too harshly.
- Confusing love and pity, which expresses itself in 'loving' people who can be pitied and rescued.
- Reacting instead of acting.

The first important thing that happens at an ACOA meeting is that people learn to break the three rules – don't talk, don't trust, don't feel – that they learned during childhood. These rules are broken by people talking about what happened in the past and what is happening now. They also access the feelings which they were never allowed to feel and to get in touch with their genuine feelings as they are today. Thirdly, they begin to trust the other people in the meeting, to respect these feelings and to treat what is being said in the meeting as confidential.

As the three rules are gradually broken, ACOAs learn to break the harmful patterns which have adversely affected their lives. These rules were necessary in childhood, for sheer survival, but they are no longer appropriate – ACOAs are no longer children suffering in alcoholic households.

In ACOA meetings, people are listened to when they talk. This is most important as, very often, these are people who have never been listened to. Gradually, members work towards accepting responsibility for themselves, and taking care of themselves rather than caring too much for other people as a way of deflecting personal problems and externalising them.

It is most important that if you suspect you may have characteristics of an Adult Child of an Alcoholic to realise that the dysfunctional behaviours you have learned for survival are in no way criticised. Nobody at an ACOA meeting is ever criticised – after all, everybody is in exactly the same boat.

Through attending ACOA meetings, you will gain the confidence to admit your powerlessness and heal the wounds which have so long interfered with adult functioning. Members must be willing to explore the origins of their childhood feelings, and to see their parents as they actually were – not as the idealised adults the children would have liked. Again, this clear-sightedness is not judgmental and does not imply criticism of the parents, but enables the feelings to come to the surface and then be dispersed.

In ACOA meetings, anonymity is preserved, and all members come for themselves, not on behalf of a friend or relative. Through the meetings, usually held once a week, people can talk freely about things they have never been able to talk about before. Nobody judges what somebody else may have done – the atmosphere engendered is one of love and acceptance.

The only 'membership' requirement is the experience of *or identification with* a compulsive or addictive family background, and a desire to become emotionally healed. All ACOAs come to understand that they lived life by certain unhealthy rules.

These included finding other compulsive personalities, and then trying to help and rescue them. ACOAs have to understand that this compounds their problems. Also, that alcoholism is basically a family disease and that family members may take on the characteristics of the disease even though they may not actually drink.

Eventually, the dysfunctional characteristics which bedevil the lives of ACOAs are reversed by healthy forms of behaviour. These include the understanding:

- That life has choices beyond mere survival.
- That there is the right to say no.
- That life motivated by fear is devoid of love and consequently empty.

At ACOA meetings, members share not only their problems but also their recovery and demonstrate to themselves and others that they can feel comfortable and involved with people and authority figures. That they can have strong personal identities and can approve of themselves. You can learn to take and use personal criticism in a positive way. You do not have to be a victim, seeking out the weak and addicted, but can become well and healthy enough to focus first and foremost on yourself.

ACOAs affirm at each meeting that in recovery they are able to stand up for themselves, that they can be peaceful and serene instead of being buffeted by uncomfortable emotions, that they can love people who are able to take care of themselves. ACOAs also give themselves permission to express their feelings, even when these may be angry and painful. They tell themselves they can have a healthy sense of self-esteem and that they are gradually learning to let go the dysfunctional patterns of behaviour learned in their families of origin.

MICHAEL'S STORY

Michael, an accountant, was in therapy for a number of psychological problems. Although his father had always been a heavy drinker, Michael did not realise this until his therapist met his father and assured him that Dad was actually a '120 carat' alcoholic.

Then things started to fall into place, My therapist sug-

gested I went to Alanon meetings, and these worked for
a bit, but after a time I felt they were not really addressing the particular problems of Adult Children.

So I joined a very new ACA meeting, and found that
this was far more what I needed. I now attend a meeting
in London for two hours each week, and the meetings
follow a set format. The list of characteristics of Adult
Children – fear of authority, abandonment, forming
relationships around addicts, rescuing people – are read
out at each meeting, and then the 12 steps.

We then read the solution to our problems, of which
the main one is to become your own loving parent – not
to expect anybody else to do this for you – and to focus
on our own inner child. After that, people will speak and
share their views, emotions and stories.

At ACA meetings, there is always a lot of emotion,
and some people find this disturbing, even frightening.
After all, we have been taught not to feel from our
earliest years. My own most difficult problem is dealing
with the denial. I find that as I strip away at one layer of
denial, there's another one underneath.

Most of us at ACA meetings are not active users of
alcohol or drugs, although many people have been chain
smokers. And although we call ourselves Adult Children
of Alcoholics, we want to get away from the idea that you
have to have an alcoholic parent in order to come along.
Any kind of dysfunctional family background is likely to
produce the recognisable characteristics.

At some stage in their lives, all Adult Children will
have been abandoned. In my case, my mother died
when I was a baby and I had a succession of nannies,
none of whom stayed long. My father remarried the
child of an alcoholic, a true codependent, and was
himself violent and abusive. As a result, I grew up
being very frightened of anger and afraid to show my
feelings.

There was also a reluctance to enter into any intimate
relationship for fear of abandonment. I've been going to
ACA meetings for about a year now, and my recovery
has progressed to the point where I am starting to be
that I have needs.

able to look after myself, to put myself first and to admit that I have needs.

Somebody who is not an Adult Child can have no idea just how difficult it is to put yourself first and take care of yourself properly. Also, I am starting to be able to experience feelings and not to be afraid of them.

Meetings of Codependents Anonymous follow pretty much the same pattern as ACOA groups, and work through a very similar recovery programme. Apart from professional therapy, which we will consider in closer detail in the following chapter, there are no other kinds of self-help groups which can aid recovery to this extent.

Even so, they are not for everybody. If, after attending one or two meetings of ACOA or CODA, you feel they are not for you, you may benefit more from professional help.

6 || Professional help

Self-help groups, where everybody is an 'expert', have proved over the years to be an excellent way of coping with codependency and related problems. For very many people, they will provide the complete answer and no actual professional help will be needed. But 12-step fellowships are not for everybody. Some people do not feel comfortable sharing their problems with a number of other fellow sufferers – or do not want to hear other people's troubles. Others perhaps are not happy with the spiritual aspects, or the mentions of God within the 12 steps. For yet others, their problems may lie too deep to be helped in this way.

At self-help fellowships, you may find that there is a tendency towards identifying with the 'average' codependent or Adult Child, to build up solidarity within the group, and end the isolation and denial which cast a shadow for so long. There is a tendency also to assume that everybody had identical problems and identical characteristics. For some, self-help groups do not distinguish well enough between people. For this reason, you may find it useful to have professional help as well, as trained therapists will treat the codependent or Adult Child as an individual with specific problems.

For example, it makes a difference whether:

- You are male or female.
- Whether you are first or last born.

110

- Whether the problems started in very early childhood or became worse as the years went by.
- Whether there was physical or sexual abuse.

Some children are more resilient than others, and even some from the same family with identical early experiences will probably have found their own personal methods of coping. Psychotherapy and counselling emphasise the importance of individual experience and pay close attention to the minutiae of family life.

The ideal is for professional help to be used as an adjunct to self-help groups, rather than replacing it altogether. But for those who simply do not like the idea, or who find they do not flourish in Anonymous-type fellowships, then professional therapy may be used on its own. There are no hard and fast rules, and for many people, finding the combination of help which suits them is a matter of trial and error.

THE ST JOSEPH'S CENTRE FOR ADDICTION

At the time of writing, the St Joseph's Centre for Addiction offers one of the most comprehensive range of professional therapies for chemically dependent and codependent people, and these can be used either by themselves or in conjuction with self-help programmes.

The Centre was first established in December, 1986, for the treatment of drug and alcohol-dependent people and their families. It is an integral part of the Holy Cross Hospital, founded in 1917 by the Congregation of the Daughters of the Cross as an independent hospital. This is a charitable, Catholic foundation in Haslemere, Surrey.

The St Joseph's project owes its inspiration to Sister Mary Agnes, who is both the Mother Superior of the Order in Haslemere, and the Matron of the hospital. For many years, the hospital had run a small detoxification unit alongside its standard hospital services, and Sister Mary Agnes had noticed a distinct pattern among patients admitted for detoxification. After drying out, many would stay for a few days until they were pronounced medically fit, and were then discharged.

Despite promises and assurances to the contrary, in very many cases, they would resume drinking very quickly, resulting in readmission to the detoxification unit some months later. Sister Mary Agnes began to feel that it was pointless to offer a service to alcohol dependent people which merely made them fit and well enough to resume their destructive behaviour. So eventually it was decided to develop a specialised intensive rehabilitation unit with the purpose of preventing the 'revolving door syndrome' of recurrent hospital admission and quick relapse.

This was done after much prayer, meditation and fund-raising by the Sisters. A senior nurse, who was herself a recovering alcoholic, was appointed as senior counsellor. For her training, she went to America to study the most effective approach yet devised for alcohol recovery, the Minnesota Model. This aims to introduce patients to the 12 steps of Alcoholics Anonymous (see Chapter 5), to offer education about the nature of addictions and their consequences, and to use group therapy to offer support and encouragement.

St Joseph's no longer conforms so strictly to the Minnesota model, although it is still used as the basis for treatment. The Centre now concentrates on the first five steps of the '12 steps,' as these have been discovered to be the most effective in this approach to substance misuse.

Significantly, the Minnesota Method involves the family in a supportive relationship. It helps families to recognise addiction as illnesses and introduces family members to the various self-help groups such as Al-Anon. It introduces a new concept known as 'tough love'. This means that family members learn not to enable by:

● Hiding bottles of drink.
● Paying for drinks.
● Picking up the consequences of the alcoholic's or addict's bad behaviour.
● Covering up or lying to conceal the truth.

As the Centre developed, it was realised that the alcohol-dependent or addicted member of the family was by no means the only one who had suffered, or reached a 'rock bottom' experience. Family members living with an active addict adapted themselves to the addictive behaviour and tried to live with it, but it became startlingly clear, when family histories were examined, that the spouse of the alcoholic or the parents of a drug addict could often identify similar patterns of behaviour in their families of origin. Either they were children of alcoholics or other shame-based family systems, and they were not new at all to the devastation caused to family life by the presence of an active addition or compulsive lifestyle. Other family members enabled, or they were workaholics, bulimics, anorexics or excessively religious, or were showing early signs of chemical dependence.

Doctors and counsellors came to realise that patterns of dysfunction around addictions were almost always multigenerational, and that it was often impossible to say: it all started here.

Working with family members, St Joseph's also soon realised that, in spite of protestations to the contrary, spouses were by no means always grateful when the drink or drug problem seemed to be solved. Originally, it was expected that they would be overwhelmed with delight when their partners were in recovery. Not a bit of it! It appeared that some families coped far better with active addiction than with recovery.

In recovery, the formerly using member often seemed to have become dull and characterless, even boring. Relationships broke up under sobriety – when they would have been expected to survive. So, almost by accident, it was realised that the non-using members often gained as much from the drinking behaviour as the addict. If things went wrong, they could be blamed on the substance. Now, in sobriety, there was nothing to blame – and yet in many cases, things still weren't right; clearly, drink was only part of a much larger problem of codependency.

Fellow sufferers in their pain and desperation were attracted to one another and codependent people were attracted to active users like iron filings to a magnet. In a sense, they couldn't choose whether to be attracted or not – codependents seemed to be propelled towards alcoholics, drug-takers, chemically dependent people of all kinds.

Gradually, a number of different treatments were developed, as it was increasingly realised that active addiction and codependency were highly complicated problems for which there could never be one overall solution. Self-help was not always the answer; psychotherapy was not always the answer. St Joseph's is now dedicated to trying to help people in the best way available and has pioneered new methods of treatment applicable to all members of the family, depending on where each one is in the process of the disease and recovery from it. Sometimes whole families can be helped, while at other times only one member is ready to receive help.

JENNY'S STORY

Jenny, for example, found that she could not seem to get anywhere in her local Adult Children of Alcoholics group.

At 23, she already had four small children. Her father was alcoholic, and had sexually and physically abused her. Following the pattern which occurs among many children of alcoholics, she had married a man who both abused and neglected her. He was a heavy drinker who behaved in an appalling way to her. He was violent to her on occasions, and at other times he would disappear for days at a time without explanation. He refused to provide sufficient money for the care of the children and would neglect to pay bills.

Realising that she needed help, she approached a local ACOA group on the recommendation of her sister, who herself was beginning to acknowledge just how much she had suffered at the hands of her father. Because her sister was doing so well at her ACOA group, Jenny decided to go along to a fellowship as well.

But she found it could not help her at all. Although she knew, to some extent, what her problems were, and wanted to speak and share her experiences with the other members, she simply could not open her mouth, and became extremely frightened. The other members of the group could sense what was the matter, but were unable to get her to open out.

Jenny's problem was that she could not feel safe in the group, yet she wanted to tell somebody her story. Eventually she approached St Joseph's and was offered individual counselling. With the help of a skilled and trained counsellor, whom she met on a once-weekly basis, she was able to speak openly about her unhappiness and began to see that she did not have to continue to live in an abusive relationship. In order to bring about change she had two options:

(1) To leave her husband, and live with her children in a women's refuge, or

(2) To confront her husband with the unacceptibility of his behaviour.

With the support of the counsellor she confronted her husband and persuaded him that if there was to be a future for their relationship there would have to be separation during which he could prove to her that he would change his behaviour and begin to be a better husband and father. Despite outbursts of anger and occasional violence and threatening behaviour, she stuck to her guns, and he eventually agreed to a period of separation. He moved out and also agreed to seek help for his problems.

At the time of writing they remain separated but see each other regularly. They have not yet resolved their differences but Jenny had made, and maintained, a very clear statement about her determination not to resume a relationship which is abusive.

Having stood up to her bullying husband she lost her fear and became able to tell her story. She tried ACOA meetings once again, and found them tremendously helpful. Now that she was at last in recovery herself, she gained insight from listening to other people's stories, and found the social contact after meetings extremely helpful while she was building her new life.

THE COUPLES IN RECOVERY GROUP

One type of professional treatment which is proving highly

successful at St Joseph's is the Couples in Recovery group, which sees couples who are already well into recovery. Although AA, Al-Anon and ACOA and CODA fellowships work extremely well, they do not offer any meeting place for couples to explore their recovery and relationship together. As all the groups essentially are for individuals, rather than to help the actual relationship, it was felt that many people could benefit from group counselling in couples, in the presence of an experienced counsellor.

It should be said here that these groups are for couples who are committed to saving their relationship – not for those considering splitting up. There is never any attempt made at St Joseph's to try and dragoon people into staying together, and sometimes it will be best for them to part. Extremely dysfunctional relationships may have no future at all. But as there is always dysfunction in any alcoholic or codependent relationship, there will be a lot of work needed, even when both partners feel the relationship is worth saving.

The Couples in Recovery groups have proved extremely popular, and are not 'anonymous' in the sense of the self-help fellowships. The groups started when one counsellor felt it would be a good idea to try to discover just how codependent relationships came about in the first place. What did these people see in each other? What attracted somebody to an alcoholic? Established at the end of 1988, these groups were the forerunners of the separate Codependency Clinic, which started in January 1990.

Only couples who are well into recovery can come to these groups, as they address often extremely painful issues, which each member of the couple has to be able to confront. The first few weeks are spent trying to establish how significant relationships have been formed from the first kiss, to first falling in love (not necessarily with the present partner), to the present relationship, to the drinking or using, recovery and beyond.

Certain specific exercises are enacted at these groups. For one, each partner is asked to introduce the other as if he/she was the other. For instance, John will introduce Mary, saying: 'I am Mary. I am short, blonde and plump and I like classical music.' The object of this exercise is to see whether the partner has any real idea of the other as a separate being, or whether they are simply imposing their wishes, likes and dislikes on to the other person. These sessions are surprisingly revealing, and they are also fun. There are a lot of laughs and jokes at the meetings, which would not be possible, probably, unless both partners were in recovery.

It usually emerges that the partners know each other far less than they imagined, even though they may have been together for 20 years or more.

Between sessions, couples are given homework to do. Communication channels are opened up which have been closed down for years, or may never have been opened up in the first place. Couples are encouraged to explore each other as though meeting a new partner. Eventually this gets to the heart of the codependency.

Relationships are examined basically from the point of view of expectations involved in getting to know somebody of the opposite sex. At the time of writing, all couples in recovery are in heterosexual relationships. It usually emerges that codependent and dysfunctional couples see the same things in each other as any other couple – when they met, each found the other exciting, attractive, fun, a character – and, significantly, they ignored the drinking or using. If ever the drinking – or chemically dependent behaviour – was noticed, there was always the expectation that through falling in love, the problem would clear up of its own accord.

In the context of codependency, people get involved in the kind of relationships that make sense to them, usually because of their backgrounds. They either feel they are not worthy of somebody who does not abuse them; or they like the idea of somebody who will devote themselves to their needs. On the surface, codependent relationships may appear much like any other – but the relationship is like a ship heading straight for an iceberg, without a compass or any other means of avoiding crashing. There is no radar, as with a healthy relationship. Until recovery, everything is in the unconscious, so there will be no recognition that this relationship is any different from any other, so that it is heading straight for the rocks.

A common pattern of the relationship is that the partners will never have been able to talk properly to one another. The group is often their first experience of hammering out problems in a satisfactory way. In the past, there will have been slights, hurts, silences, rages – but never any real communication.

It can be the case that neither partner is abusing alcohol or any other substance at the time of the marriage. Then, gradually, over the years, difficulties with drink develop – and the codependency of the other partner may well develop in response to this. Overwhelmingly, alcoholics – even incipient alcoholics – seek out codependent partners, and this pattern will continue until the denial can be dropped. Couples in Recovery groups are for those who have already started to shed the denial – otherwise, they cannot be helped in this way.

The couples groups are important, because major problems often occur when one family member is in recovery and, for the first time, starts to see things as they are. The scales have fallen from the recovering partner's eyes – but not necessarily from those around, who carry on in the same way as before.

In intimate relationships, as you may already have discovered, if one partner is not ready, then there is not much that the other can do. It's a bit like trying to make somebody give up smoking. Smokers know that the habit is bad for them, that they risk getting cancer and other diseases if they don't give up. But if someone comes along, hides their cigarettes, says how dreadful they are to continue smoking rather than give up – then the feeling is: why don't they go away and mind their own business? Couples cannot be helped together unless there is an equal commitment on both sides – and this is very often not the case.

RECOVERY AND DISCOVERY

The effect that the recovery of one partner may have on the other is exemplified by the story of Jean and Ray.

Jean, 43, fell in love with Ray, 45, 13 years ago. They had a wonderful whirlwind romance and were married three months after their first meeting. Jean had been aware when they met that Ray drank too much, and she also knew that his behaviour was moody and unpredictable during drinking bouts. Like most codependents, however, she hoped that her love would soon change him and encourage him to become sober. It had the exact opposite effect, and the drinking got steadily worse. Jean tried to cover up for him, and held on to the belief that in the end, her love would overcome the problem.

As Ray's drinking got steadily worse, Jean came to feel that God was somehow punishing her for some sin she had committed – although she couldn't think what it could be. In her friends' and neighbours' eyes, she was seen as a selfless martyr, and she rather enjoyed this new status.

Then Ray agreed to undergo in-patient treatment. (Withdrawal from severe alcoholism can be very dangerous without proper medical supervision, and those who have been regularly using large quantities of alcohol can often need in-patient treatment in a hospital.) The treatment proved a success and Jean expected the relationship would recover. Unfortunately this did not happen.

The trouble was that when Ray was in recovery, the relationship seemed shallow and unexciting compared to how it was before. A computer engineer, he worked hard to pay off all the debts that had accumulated during his alcoholism, when his life had become unmanageable. Like so many addicts, where the underlying codependency remains untreated, he substituted one dependency for another and, in recovery from alcoholism, became a workaholic.

Ray had joined AA and Jean went along to Al-Anon meetings, on the same Wednesday, and at the same time. They found that the only time they talked was on the 10-minute journey to and from meetings. All their other time seemed to be taken up with Ray's job and Jean's voluntary and school governor work.

After discussing their new situation, both decided to try a Couples in Recovery group, through which the true dynamics of the relationship were eventually understood and their problems resolved.

Jean was the youngest of five sisters. At puberty, she had been discovered in her parents' bed by her mother, who was shocked to find her husband fondling Jean's nipples. There was an almighty row, during which Jean's mother demanded that Jean and her father should never again be alone together. Jean and her father complied with this restriction and there were no further incidents of this kind.

But inwardly, Jean was devastated by what had happened. She blamed herself, feeling that she must have been inappropriately seductive and, as a result, came to sense danger in any intimate relationship with a man.

As she grew up, she came to feel that because of her 'dirtiness' it was best to keep relationships with men at a distance. Ray seemed to be the perfect partner; she knew unconsciously that because of his drinking, he would never get uncomfortably close to her. Therefore, her secret 'badness' would never be discovered.

When Ray stopped drinking, Jean became frightened, because for the first time in their marriage, he was able to get close to her. This brought her closer to the pain of her inner sense of shame, and the feeling of guilt and responsibility for what had happened between her and her father. She felt, unconsciously, that she might damage her parents if ever the truth came out and it was discovered that her father, not she, was responsible for the inappropriate sexual behaviour.

When all this had come out into the open, initially, there was deep sadness at the loss of her 'wonderful' father, and her capacity to trust her parents. But Jean was able to get closer to her husband because she was able to get close to herself, and access those painful memories from the past.

Although Jean benefited greatly from the Couples in Recovery group, when the first hint of her sexual abuse came out, it became necessary for her to have a few sessions of one-to-one therapy with a counsellor who understood child sexual abuse.

Sexual abuse can be a feature in these codependency situations. Usually, the victim has consciously forgotten all about it, and it may not come out for very many sessions. When it does, the person in recovery has to get to the point where she or he accepts that it was not their fault, and they were not responsible.

Some sexual abusers claim that they could not help what they did because the child was seductive. This is the motif in the famous novel *Lolita*, and led to the nymphet tag, where young girls of 11 or 12 were seen as deliberately making themselves sexy-looking. But, even if children do behave seductively, this never gives an adult in a position of responsibility licence to act sexually. It's rubbish for the perpetrator to say that he or she was only responding to what the child wanted. Adults are supposed to know better, however the child might behave.

Several give-away signs indicate early sexual abuse. You may experience extreme difficulties with touching, with intimate relationships, with being physical in any way – these are all intimations. We are only now realising just how common sexual abuse is, and the significant part it can play in the development of codependency. If it happened to you, take courage from the fact that help is now available – and seek it out by contacting one of the organisations mentioned at the end of this book.

THE SEXUALITY IN RECOVERY GROUP

This was established at St Joseph's in response to the numbers of chemically dependent women who had been sexually abused in childhood. Sexual abuse is less common in codependency than emotional abuse, but even so, it is common enough.

The point about the Sexuality in Recovery group is that women (the usual victims, although men can also suffer) enter periods of profound regression when memories of abusive relationships, long buried, rise to the surface. This group helps victims to face up to the trauma, and to understand that it was not their fault. Sexual abuse is never the victim's fault, but it almost always leads such people as adults to form dysfunctional relationships with other adults. Until the problem is addressed, the pattern will be endlessly repeated, with women asking themselves: Why do I always seem to attract such abusive men? – yet not being able to find the answer. The answer always lies in coming from the types of background described throughout this book.

AUTOBIOGRAPHY WORK

This was developed in response to the many people who contact St Joseph's but who live too far away to come to the Centre on a regular basis. Writing an autobiography is, for some people, a vital way of recovering, as it helps them to remember where the trouble started, and to understand why there may be large gaps in their conscious memories.

With autobiography work, which often proceeds by correspondence, at least initially, lives are taken in 10-year chunks.

This is not fast, instant therapy but may take weeks or even months to complete. Partly, of course, length of therapy depends on the age of the patient – a 60-year-old's autobiography will most probably take longer than a 20-year-old's. When each 10-year period has been covered, the writer sends a photocopy to the therapist and they arrange to meet and talk over the feelings which have been released in the process of writing. What has been left out is often as relevant as what is included.

Generally speaking, autobiography work takes about six months to complete, and, like the other therapies, it may be extremely painful. People have no idea when they start writing what will come up, and often it is very important to have trained support to cope with and understand the feelings that emerge. (It's not unusual for writers to experience very strong feelings at times, when painful memories rise up out of the unconscious.)

Most people imagine that their families of origin were loving and supportive and are often very surprised to find they have very ambivalent feelings about their hitherto idealised parents. Usually, if they can remember very little about certain points of their childhood, this means they have blanked out.

Although at first autobiography work was devised as a means of getting those who live far way to have access to therapy, this method is becoming so successful that it is now also used for patients who can easily attend the Clinic for treatment.

FAMILY THERAPY

St Joseph's employs three family therapists on a sessional basis to work with the families, where appropriate, of clients who are undergoing treatment in the residential chemical dependency programme. (See below.)

CHEMICAL DEPENDENCY TREATMENT PROGRAMME

St Joseph's offers a six- to ten-week intensive residential programme for chemical dependency. The treatment programme places the 12-step programme of Alcoholics Anonymous at the centre of its philosophy. It also fully acknowledges the central role of codependency in understanding and treating chemical dependency. The following letter relates the experience of one man who left the centre in July 1990:

When I arrived at St Joe's, I had already decided that the duration of my stay would be measured in days – in, dry out, and out. When they talked of changing my life, I met this with complete denial. No one or nothing could alter me because I'm different from everyone else and no one really understands me anyway. So what's the use? After all, I'm not really an addict and alcoholic. I can control it. I can stop on my own. I don't need this, I'm not into God and religion. What a sound attitude I had, one that was guaranteed to keep me using the drug of my choice. After a week and writing a life story, I began to think, 'OK, maybe I have a bit of a problem, but it's not that bad'. Well, it was and the following weeks opened up my mind a bit more. I resisted, deflected. I was aggressive, abusive, the lot – but deep down something kept me here. I knew they were right, that the alcohol and drugs were the symptom. What caused me to use in the first place and kept me using was the problem. I discovered feelings I thought I never had. I learned how to accept love and care from others but most of all I learned how to trust. I discovered I was a child who had suffered inside me, carrying the pain, the grief, the shame and the guilt which was killing me. The little me who wants to live, the child within. It wasn't easy. When the going got tough, the tough stayed. I faced me. My higher power had found me and I him, my life, my attitude and the emptiness inside me began to fill. The 12-step programme will work if you work it. It's simple. But no one said it was easy. Hang on to honesty – it's a key. Hang on to hope – it's your passport. Hang on to faith to become 'real' and you will. I did.

Thank you for my life.

A very grateful member,

Frank M

OTHER PROFESSIONAL HELP

We have described the various clinics and therapies available at St Joseph's because one of us – David Stafford – knew the set up there and because, in many ways, this Centre has pioneered professional codependency treatment. But that does not mean everybody has to go to St Joseph's in order to be treated successfully for this condition. There are many therapists who, while perhaps not being aware of the use of the definition of *codependency*, will recognise the condition instantly once it has been explained. Only the word is new – the concepts have been in our culture for centuries, even if it is only now that it is being realised that such relationships arise from dysfunctional patterns rather than healthy ones.

John Bowlby, who propounded the famous 'attachment' theory, wrote as long ago as the 1940s that much adult pathology had its origins in family interactions. In his work, he describes how some parents invert the natural child-parent relationship by requiring the child to be the parent, and adopting the role of the child. As a rule, said Bowlby, this inversion is camouflaged, so that it masquerades as something else – the pretence, usually, of the happy, well-adjusted family.

Bowlby also understood that when the parent becomes the child, with desperate needs, the child cannot grow up to be autonomous. He says: 'Unknown to herself, mother (or father) is seeking belated satisfaction of her desire for the loving care she either never had as a child, or perhaps lost.'

FAMILY THERAPY

This type of treatment is available at many Centres (including St Joseph's) and is well established. Although many family therapists may not have come across the word codependency, they will understand that the dynamics of dysfunction are usually multi-generational. What family therapists may not appreciate, however, is the effect that chemical dependency may have on family problems.

Many family therapists take the view that if the underlying family dynamics can change, then the addiction will tend to disappear of its own accord. Those who have worked with chemically dependent people know that this is not true – the addiction has to be addressed first and foremost, and no healing can take place until there is recovery from the addiction. Where there is serious chemical dependency, it may be difficult to get effective help from a family therapist, unless it is understood that addiction is a progressive disease which will never get better by itself.

If there is no chemical dependency, or substance abuse, then family therapy can be extremely effective for addressing codependency patterns.

Family therapists tend to be already professionally trained as doctors, psychologists or social workers before undertaking family therapy training. Most usually, therapists will see couples together, and they will want to meet with the whole family at some stage. In some cases, family therapy is available in Britain under the NHS.

PSYCHOTHERAPY

There are many different kinds of psychotherapy. In the psychoanalytic field there are Jungian, Freudian, Kleinian and the British School of psychoanalysis. We don't propose to examine in any detail the different schools here, but the following is a very crude guide.

Jungians emphasise the collective unconscious and spiritual experience. Freudians concentrate on sexuality, and its development as the core of personality. Kleinians pay great attention to earliest infantile development and the aggressive impulses. The British School emphasises environmental factors in development. Because of this the psychotherapist who adheres to the British School is probably best equipped to help with problems of codependency, but there can be no hard and fast rules about these things and most psychoanalytically trained psychotherapists of whatever school will be helpful.

People will usually see a psychotherapist alone, and sessions will take place at least twice weekly for several months. All psychoanalytically trained psychotherapists will have been in treatment themselves before attempting to treat others.

In the field of humanistic psychotherapy codependents may find psychodrama (re-enacting traumatic events) and guided fantasy work (visualisations) helpful in their search to become whole people once again.

SPECIALISED CHEMICAL DEPENDENCY COUNSELLORS

These people are specifically trained to bring the chemically dependent into recovery, and assist those who have experienced a relapse. They also encourage those who are finding the early stages of recovery extremely difficult.

Almost all these counsellors will be alcoholics or addicts in recovery themselves, which means they have intimate personal experience of the problems they are trying to help.

SPECIALISED CODEPENDENCY COUNSELLORS

This is a small but growing field. Codependency counsellors, like chemical dependency counsellors, have been through the mill themselves, and have undertaken training in order to help others to recognise and address this problem.

GUIDELINES FOR THE CHEMICALLY DEPENDENT

Those who recognise a chemical dependency problem in themselves must address this problem before attempting codependency treatment. The first thing is to go to your local AA or NA (Narcotics Anonymous) group, as they will know how to advise and support you.

It is important to understand that if you have been drinking heavily and consistently over a number of years you will need medical help to detoxify. Otherwise, there may be severe delusional states connected with withdrawal or, worse still, potentially lethal fits. It is also a good idea to go to your GP to see whether any other physical damage had been caused by the drinking, for example, to the liver.

There are not usually medical risks involved in stopping opiate use, but some people find it helpful to have medical assistance in the form of 'chemical cushions' – drugs which offset the discomfort of the withdrawal process.

Withdrawal from tranquillisers or other prescribed drugs should be done gradually and, ideally, also under medical supervision. You will also almost certainly need psychological support towards the end of the withdrawal period, as panic attacks and other frightening withdrawal symptoms are common.

If you are recommended for more intensive treatment, either because the above methods have not worked or because the addiction has progressed beyond the point where it can be treated on an out-patient basis, it may be necessary to go into hospital or a specialised treatment centre. The method with the most consistent record for success in in-patient treatment is the Minnesota Model, based on the 12 steps described in Chapter 5, and with complete abstinence as its goal.

We do not recommend controlled drinking or methadone programmes as, although they may stabilise the substance use, they will also stabilise the dysfunction in personal relationships – so no real healing can take place. It also seems that unless substance use has ceased, psychotherapy and counselling have extremely limited value. They can, indeed, have the effect of shoring up defensive systems, papering over the cracks, rather than getting to the heart of the problem and tackling it at source.

Note: at the moment, anybody can set up as a counsellor, therapist or psychologist without having any training or skills at all. Because of this, if you feel you have a serious codependency problem for which you would like to find help, do not start looking in Yellow Pages or respond to people who advertise their services. Although some people who advertise may be excellent, the risk is too great to take. There are recognised training schools which ensure professionals undergo proper training and competence assessment. If you are not sure when booking up a therapist, ask what training they have had and which professional body they belong to. A resource list is given on pages 137–139.

FAMILY DOCTOR HELP

At the moment, very few family doctors know anything about codependency, or can recognise it in their patients.

One of the most common manifestations of codependency is depression, for which anti-depressants will frequently be prescribed. of course, they cannot cure the problem, but that does not mean they do not have a place. In some severe cases, a short course of anti-depressants or tranquillisers can enable people to relax enough in order to be able to listen to therapists, or to attend a self-help group. But of course, no drugs can every truly help the codependency – as they will still be medicating the pain, and the important thing is to become free of all chemical props.

Those lucky enough to have a family doctor who understands the complicated issues connected with codependency can gain valuable help by combining attendance at a self-help group with continuing to see the doctor, as progress can then be monitored by an outside agent. In some cases, the codependency may be at least partly causing an actual illness, such as M.E., chronic backache or lowered immunity to infection. In such cases, it may be important to continue with medical treatment for the physical condition. Self-help groups will not necessarily be enough to treat actual medical conditions.

‖ SUMMING UP

Codependency is an extremely common condition which, from time to time, touches us all. The majority of us never achieve complete detachment, complete independence from other people, or total separation from roles and relationships. But in healthy relationships, codependency will never predominate.

Problems arise when the condition is present to such an extent that satisfactory relationships are no longer possible for us, and where codependency characterises our whole behaviour and relationships with others.

The underlying cause of codependency is alienation from the self, coupled with feelings of low self-worth and low self-esteem. The emptiness inside, which leads us to pretence and denial of genuine emotions, can in time cause depression, physical illnesses and compulsive behaviour such as drinking, gambling, sexaholism, churchaholism, love and relationship addictions, if we do not seek help.

The esteem which should come from within is externalised, so that it can only be gained vicariously. A codependent wife lives through her husband; a codependent doctor lives through his work. Take away the husband, or the medical practice – and what is left? If there is serious codependency, the answer often seems to be – nothing.

Intensive research has revealed that codependency stems from a deep-rooted fear of abandonment, which leads to an excessive need to control and dominate and is then responsible for unsatisfactory relationships with other people. Codependents need to control others because they fear they cannot control themselves. It seems so much easier to try and impose one's will on another person. And as this book has shown, there are many ways of imposing one's will, and not all are immediately apparent.

DENIAL AND CONCEALMENT

The sternly dominating and rigid father, husband or schoolteacher are obvious examples. But people can dominate just as surely through illness, through manipulative and seductive wiles, through pathetic, non-coping behaviour and even through excessive kindness and apparent saintliness.

Codependency comes in many guises, and may be very well concealed because, above all, it is a disease of denial. Codependents are usually inwardly ashamed of themselves, because unconsciously they believe they are unworthy, and they will resort to many tricks and rationalisations to conceal these feelings. An excessively codependent mother, for example, may excuse her behaviour by saying: 'You never stop worrying about your children, do you?' – as if this is not only completely normal, but integral to being a good mother.

A wife who 'does everything' for her husband – packing his case, picking up his dirty underwear off the floor, or getting out of bed at one in the morning to cook him a meal, may tell friends: 'Of course, George is so useless, like a child, really.'

The more powerful or elevated the husband is in society, the more likely she is to say this. Of course, the same can happen the other way round, but it's less common for husbands to look after their wives in this way. So many women have been trained from birth for codependency – so much so that it is often the expected behaviour, and a non-codependent woman will tend to be seen by others as 'hard' or 'unfeeling', or 'unnatural'.

Nobody is to blame for codependency, however. It seems almost certain that the condition is caused by growing up in the type of family where parents are never really there for the children, but instead the children are there for the parents.

The need and wish to idealise the parents tends to make children from these dysfunctional families blame themselves for the abuse, the alcoholism, drug-taking, or even the coldness and withdrawal – whichever happens to be the way in which the dysfunction manifests itself.

According to our definitions, then, all families are disfunctional to some extent. Undoubtedly yours will have been. But not all families produce emotionally disabled codependents. The families where codependency flourishes are those where there is a pretence that everything is all right, where nothing real is ever discussed or explained to the children and where, nevertheless, there is a pretence that this is a happy, normal family. Even when this pretence cannot be maintained by the adults, the children will do their best to make out that their home life is perfect. As children they are never allowed to be themselves, but always feel they must play a part, whether this is of mother's little helper, the rescuer, or the scapegoat, the hero or the 'lost child', and so they continue playing this part – or parts – into adulthood. Do you identify with this pattern?

REPEATING THE PATTERN

The saddest aspect of codependency is that such children almost invariably repeat the pattern of their own childhood. Or they attempt to do the opposite, in revenge, to show their parents that they can do better. Perhaps that has been your reaction.

Sometimes, we may become so successful at playing a part that nobody ever guesses what goes on underneath. But always, we experience also the fear of one day going out of control. And, like any other addiction, codependency is progressive. Unless it is addressed, it will get worse – and be passed on to the next generation.

In codependent families, denial and pretence have become the standard ways of relating. This leads to a rigid rule system being established, where all family members know that certain subjects, certain feelings, are taboo. So they are internalised, repressed. If you have been raised in such an environment you no doubt learned that you don't talk, don't trust, and don't feel.

It is just possible that codependency may have some genetic base, as alcoholism seems to have. But it is far more likely to be transmitted through social interaction within the family, eventually becoming a way of relating to everybody, not just family members. Codependents simply don't know any other ways of relating.

ROAD TO RECOVERY

Addiction studies have shown that all forms of compulsive behaviour – eating disorders, compulsive gambling, sexaholism, alcoholism, spendaholism – are external manifestations of underlying codependency. This is why the codependency must be treated as well as the actual addiction. Otherwise, true recovery is never possible.

Nobody should ever think that codependency, as defined in this book, is normal behaviour. It is essentially *learned* behaviour, a survival mechanism, a reaction to a bad situation, and as such can (and should) be unlearned.

Fortunately, it is possible to recover from codependency, and many of us can achieve this without any professional help, simply by joining a relevant self-help group such as Codependents Anonymous or Adult Children of Alcoholics. (You do not have to have been an actual child of an alcoholic to go to one of these groups – it is enough to recognise yourself as a codependent, whatever kind of family dysfunction brought this about.)

At self-help groups, which are run entirely by and for sufferers, with no 'professional' being present, the process of recovery comes about by learning to break those old-established but no longer relevant, rigid family rules. The denial and pretence are addressed, and replaced by honesty, openness and mutual support. Gradually, the frozen emotions inside you begin to thaw, and rigid, addictive ways of relating to other people are replaced by the ability to form healthy relationships, based on mutual regard and respect – love with detachment rather than clinginess, neediness and addiction. Most codependents in recovery discover that they now attract, and are attracted by a different kind of person. Just as one codependent attracts another, so in recovery there will be attraction to those who are healthy, and not codependent.

Many codependents have a history of poor relationships which always seem to go wrong, however well they started out. Sometimes, through recovery, it will be possible to rescue a relationship which has become submerged in codependent, addictive behaviour. For others, it may be necessary to seek new relationships, new jobs.

It should be said that recovery from codependency sometimes imposes severe strains on existing relationships. After all, the people surrounding a codependent will have got used to a certain type of behaviour, and may feel resentful when it is no longer there. A husband may be initially dismayed when his wife is no longer willing to pick up his discarded clothes or tidy the bathroom after him. A boss may not like it when a previously willing secretary now requests overtime when asked to stay late.

Recovery may not always be comfortable at first for the other people in one's life. But it is always worth it because, actually, nobody ever respects a 'doormat'.

PROFESSIONAL HELP

Sometimes, complete recovery through a self-help group is not possible without professional help. If this proves to be so in your case, do not despair. Nowadays, there are therapists and counsellors trained in codependency treatment – almost always people who have been through a traumatic mill themselves and who understand the condition backwards – available as back-up to the self-help groups.

For best results, any professional help should be carried out in conjunction with an appropriate Anonymous group.

You will know that you are recovering when, possibly for the first time, you are able to make choices based on your own needs and wishes, and are not driven by desperate compulsion to do things which go against your natural inclination. You are recovering when your life is not governed by an overwhelming need to please other people, and when love is no longer confused with need.

In a non-codependent relationship, each partner is free to

breathe and does not feel joined at the hip to the other. The new feeling of inner security means that the sense of happiness can come from within, rather than being dependent on the behaviour or inclinations of others.

Recovery means that you are no longer a prisoner of the past. You have been able to break free – and live your own life, as *you* want to live it.

Resource list

Self-help groups

The following self-help groups have national offices which can be contacted for information about local groups in your area.

Alcoholics Anonymous
PO Box 1
Stonebow House
Stonebow
York
YO1 2NJ
Tel: 01904 644026

London Service Office
Tel: 0171-352 3001

AA offers advice and information to problem drinkers. The only criteria for using an AA group is that you are a problem drinker with a desire to stop drinking.

Narcotics Anonymous
UK Service Office,
202 City Road
London EC1V 2PH
Tel: 0171-730 0009

NA offers advice and information to problem illicit or prescribed drug users. The only criteria for using an NA group is that you are a problem drug user with a desire to stop.

Al-Anon Family Groups
61 Great Dover Street
London SE1 4YF
Tel: 0171-403 0888

Al-Anon offers advice and information to family members or friends of problem drinkers. The only criteria for using an Al-Anon group is that your life brings you into contact with a problem drinker. Ala-Teen is a special group for teenagers where a parent is a problem drinker.

Families Anonymous
The Doddington & Rolo's Community Association
Charlotte Despard Avenue, London SW11 5JE
Tel: 0171-498 4680

FA offers advice and information to family members or friends of problem drug takers. The only criteria for using an FA group is that your life brings you into contact with a problem drug taker.

Codependents Anonymous
PO Box 1292
London N4 2YX

CODA is for anyone who recognises a problem of codependency and is seeking to grow from it.

Adult Children of Alcoholics Al-Anon (ACOA) or ACA
c/o National Association for Children of Alcoholics
PO Box 52
Haslemere
Surrey
GU27 1JA
Tel: 0800 838 597

ACOA or ACA is for anyone who recognises the impact of growing up in a family with a parent who is alcoholic, or for those who can identify similar dysfunctional patterns in their family of origin, and wish to grow from them. Anyone who is codependent for whatever reason can use ACOA or ACA.

General information and advice

The National Association for Children of Alcoholics
PO Box 52
Haslemere
Surrey
GU27 1JA
Tel: 0800 838 597

NACOA is a charity which has four broad aims: raising the profile of children of alcoholics (COAs) in the public consciousness; reaching professionals who deal with COAs in their everyday work and educating them as to the needs of COAs; offering advice, information, and fellowship to COAs; promoting research into the phenomena of COAs.

Professional services

St Joseph's Centre for Addiction
Holy Cross Hospital
Hindhead Road
Haslemere
Surrey
GU27 1NQ
Tel: 01428 656517

St Joseph's offers a comprehensive range of services to drug and alcohol dependent people and their families, including detoxification and in-patient rehabilitation. The Co-dependency Clinic is an out-patient service offering help to codependent people whether or not drugs or alcohol are involved.

The Chemical Dependency Centre
11 Redcliffe Gardens
London SW10 9BG
Tel: 0171-352 2552

CDC run an out-patient clinic offering assessment, diagnosis and referral, individual counselling, group therapy, and after-care, for chemically dependent people. Services are provided regardless of whether patients can pay for them or not.

Arbours Consultation Service
6 Church Lane
London N8 7BU
Tel: 0181-348 6466

The Arbours Consultation Service offers assessment for psychotherapy and referral to trained and experienced psychotherapists. There is a low-cost psychotherapy service where patients are seen by student psychotherapists under supervision from experienced psychotherapists. This service *is not suitable for those who are chemically dependent.*

Westminster Pastoral Foundation
23 Kensington Square
London W8 5HN
Tel: 0171-937 6956

WPF offers an excellent counselling service to a wide range of people with various problems. It also has associated counselling services in many parts of the country. WPF trained counsellors tend to be of a high quality. This service *is not suitable for those who are chemically dependent.*

Further reading

Codependent No More by Melody Beattie, Hazelden, 1987.

Children of Alcoholics by David Stafford, Piatkus, 1992.

Children of Light, Children of Denial by Lynn Buess, Light Technology, Sedona, 1989.

Codependent's Guide to the Twelve Steps by Melody Beattie, Piatkus, 1990.

Painful Affairs: Looking for Love through Addiction and Codependency by Joseph R. Cruse, MD Health Communications Ltd, Florida, 1989.

Smart Love. A recovery programme based on the experiences of the *Women Who Love Too Much* groups, by Judy Hayes, Arrow, 1990.

How to Combat Anorexia, Bulimia and Compulsive Overeating: the Promis Handbook on Eating Disorders and Recovery by Dr Robert Lefever, Promis Books, 1988.

The Drama of Being a Child by Alice Miller, Virago, 1987.

For Your Own Good by Alice Miller, Virago, 1987.

Women Who Love Too Much by Robin Norwood, Arrow, 1986

In case of difficulty in obtaining any of these books, contact:

Compendium Bookshop
234 Camden High Street
London NW1 8QS
Tel: 0171-485 8944

‖ INDEX

143